A Short History of Carson City

T0288336

A SHORT HISTORY OF

Carson City

RICHARD MORENO

UNIVERSITY OF NEVADA PRESS   RENO & LAS VEGAS

University of Nevada Press, Reno, Nevada 89557 USA
Copyright © 2011 by University of Nevada Press
All rights reserved
Manufactured in the United States of America
Design by Kathleen Szawiola

Library of Congress Cataloging-in-Publication Data

Moreno, Richard.
A short history of Carson City / Richard Moreno.
    p. cm.
Includes bibliographical references and index.
ISBN 978-0-87417-836-4 (pbk. : alk. paper)
1. Carson City (Nev.)—History. I. Title.
F849.C3M67 2011
979.3'57—dc22   2010042828

The paper used in this book is a recycled stock made from 30 percent post-consumer waste materials, certified by FSC, and meets the requirements of American National Standard for Information Sciences—Permanence of Paper for Printed Library Materials, ANSI/NISO Z39.48-1992 (R2002). Binding materials were selected for strength and durability.

FRONTISPIECE:
Carson City's streets and buildings were draped with patriotic banners, signs, and flags during President Theodore Roosevelt's visit to the capital city, 1903. (Special Collections, University of Nevada, Reno Libraries)

This book has been reproduced as a digital reprint.

TO BARBARA AND MYRICK LAND

Contents

Preface

*C*arson City owes a lot to its location. Situated nearly at the midpoint between Virginia City, Reno, and Lake Tahoe, Carson City is the nexus of northern Nevada. Its position on the map allowed it to be the logical link between Comstock mines, Reno railroads, and Tahoe timber and water. It also owes much to a transplanted New Yorker named Abraham Curry, who figured that if he donated a chunk of undeveloped land in the center of the city it might entice the territorial (and later, state) leaders to place the seat of government in the community and thereby ensure its long-term success and prosperity.

Ironically, Carson City's location also attracted me—a transplanted Californian—to relocate there in the early 1980s. I was looking to buy my first house and Carson City not only offered less-expensive prices than Reno or Sparks but also was closer to where I worked at the time. It was while living in Carson City that I was invited to write a weekly travel-history column for the *Nevada Appeal* that led to my first two books, published by the Children's Museum of Northern Nevada. Carson City is also where I met my wife and where my daughter was born. You could say that I owe a lot to Carson City.

When my friends Myrick and Barbara Land originally wrote *A Short History of Reno,* they were looking for a publisher and I suggested the University of Nevada Press. It turned out to be a successful partnership with the Press, and they followed up with *A Short History of Las Vegas*. A few years later, after Mike's untimely passing and Barbara had moved to Illinois to be closer to family, I was rereading their Reno book and had a thought—what about continuing their series of short history books to include Carson City? The idea seemed to have merit particularly since there are only a handful of history books about the capital city. So I received Barbara's blessing and approached the University of Nevada Press, which gave it the green light.

It's my hope that this little book will help repay that debt I owe to Mr. Curry's town.

LIKE ANY BOOK, this work owes much to a number of people who generously provided help during its preparation. I would like to thank Guy Louis Rocha for his tireless hunt for the truth in history and for being a good friend—this book could not have been possible without his helpful suggestions and corrections. I would also like to thank Liz Moore at the Nevada State Archives, Joel Guldner of the University of Nevada, Reno Special Collections, Julie Duewel at the Nevada Department of Transportation, and Delsye Mills and Diane Rush of the Carson-Tahoe Hospital Auxiliary for their help in locating photos. I also need to thank Scott Schrantz for his advice on historic details; Charlie Johnston of *Nevada Magazine* for his last-minute help; Joanne O'Hare, director of the University of Nevada Press, who believed in this project from the very beginning; my editor, Matt Becker, for his encouragement and support; Isabel Espinoza for helping locate the oral history of JohnD and Kay Winters; and Barbara Land and her late husband, Myrick, for the wonderful example they set as journalists and teachers, and for creating the short history model. Lastly, I would like to offer a special thanks to my wife, Pam, for supporting my writing efforts, and to my children, Hank and Julia, for patiently listening when I needed to sound out ideas or bored them with some new historical information.

A Short History of Carson City

Introduction

By and by Carson City was pointed out to us. It nestled in the edge of a great plain and was a sufficient number of miles away to look like an assemblage of mere white spots in the shadow of a grim range of mountains overlooking it, whose summits seemed lifted clearly out of companionship and consciousness of earthly things. —MARK TWAIN, Roughing It *(1869)*

*C*arson City's past speaks through its historic houses and buildings. Unlike many Western American cities, which subscribe to a newer-must-be-better philosophy and demolish any home or business that is more than twenty-five years old, Carson City has attempted to preserve its most historical structures. While many, like the original Virginia & Truckee Railroad maintenance shops, Chinatown, and the Nevada State Children's Home, have been lost over the years, it is still possible, in the older sections of the city, to find dozens of charming dwellings and businesses constructed in a variety of classic architectural styles from Victorian to Romanesque to Gothic Revival. The different architectural designs not only reflect what was popular at various times but serve as a road map for how Carson City developed and grew.

Indeed, the best way to learn about Carson City is to wander the town's downtown and neighborhoods, particularly on the west side, which acclaimed Nevada author Robert Laxalt, who grew up in Carson City, once described as "the high-toned part of town, spreading down from the Governor's Mansion. Its gracious lawns and flower gardens lay under a canopy of cottonwood trees." Pass by the brick, stone, and wooden buildings and listen closely, for they speak volumes about a community that can trace its roots to Nevada's earliest days. Not surprisingly, several years ago the city's convention and visitors bureau concocted a walking tour of the area—called the Kit Carson Trail—that is marked by a bright blue line painted on the sidewalks. Loosely modeled after Boston's Freedom Trail, the Kit Carson tour follows a two-and-a-half-mile path that meanders by several dozen historic structures, including the State Capitol and the Governor's Mansion.

A stroll on the trail, in fact, serves as a virtual primer on Carson City history. While you can join the trail at any point, perhaps the most logical place to start is at the State Capitol, a smallish—compared to some other statehouses—but elegant gray-brown sandstone structure erected between 1870 and 1871. Reflecting the styles of the day, its design incorporates Renaissance Revival and Italianate elements. The Capitol is essential to Carson City's sense of self; it is what defines the city and makes it different from its larger sister communities. Las Vegas may have a pyramid, a volcano, a faux Eiffel Tower, and the Stratosphere Tower—and Reno has its Arch and National Bowling Center—but only Carson City is the state capital and the seat of government for Nevada.

Across Carson Street from the Capitol is a trio of classic, pillared structures designed to look appropriately weighty and substantial: the Neoclassical Heroes Memorial Building, home of the Nevada Attorney General, the former Carson City/Ormsby County Courthouse, and the former Nevada Supreme Court Building, built in the Moderne style. These halls of justice, built between 1920 and 1936, reflect a time when Nevada was finally able to sink down permanent roots and move beyond its hardscrabble past as a transient mining state that some felt did not belong in the fraternity of American states.

If you slip behind the phalanx of legal buildings and continue north on Curry Street, there is the Edward D. Sweeney Building (102 South Curry), an important commercial structure in early Carson City. According to retired Nevada state archivist Guy Louis Rocha, Orion Clemens (older brother of Samuel Clemens [Mark Twain] and former secretary of the Nevada Territory) was among its first occupants. Additionally, it served as office space for Nevada's first governor, Henry Blasdel. Peter Cavanaugh, Sweeney's father-in-law and a local contractor who also built the State Capitol, erected this two-story brick building in 1864. Today, the building serves as an art and antiques shop.

One of Carson City's oldest structures is the Edward D. Sweeney Building (102 South Curry), erected in 1864. (Richard Moreno)

A half-block north is the majestic Mathias Rinckel Mansion (102 North Curry), a grand Italianate-style home constructed in 1875–76 for a local butcher, who made a fortune supplying meat to Virginia City miners and Lake Tahoe lumbermen. Rinckel equipped his house with state-of-the-art kitchen and laundry devices and filled it with fine imported furnishings. Today, it is used for offices.

Another block west is Nevada Street, which, as you continue north, passes the quaint Benjamin H. Meder home (308 North Nevada), built in about 1875 for a prominent businessman who was also a longtime Ormsby County commissioner and state senator. It continues to be a private home. A half block farther north (406 North Nevada) is Carson City founder Abraham Curry's former home, erected in 1871. Curry used sandstone quarried from the Nevada State Prison (he served as

the prison warden from 1862 to 1864) to construct his solid, single-story abode. The home originally boasted a large front porch as well as an octagonal cupola that served as a skylight for the dining room. These days, it serves as a suite of offices.

Next door to the Curry place is the elegant Alfred Chartz House (412 North Nevada). Built in 1876, it was acquired by Chartz, a prominent mining and water rights lawyer, in 1894. His story is even more remarkable because he served eight years in prison for shooting a man. In the early 1870s, Chartz worked at an eastern Nevada newspaper. One day, his editor was threatened by another man and Chartz, thinking the man was armed, pulled out his own gun and shot the man. He was sentenced to life imprisonment but was pardoned in 1882.

From there, if you turn left on West Spear Street and right on Division Street, you reach the Orion Clemens House (502 North Division). The elder Clemens constructed this ten-room stucco house (the exterior has been modified over the years) in 1863, when he served as the first and only secretary of the Nevada Territory. It's believed that his brother Sam Clemens stayed in the home periodically in 1864. In the mid-twentieth century, the house was converted into offices.

At the end of the block is the Henry M. Yerington House (512 North Division). A local lawyer, Thomas Haydon, built the central part of the house in 1863. Six years later, Yerington, general manager of the Virginia and Truckee Railroad, purchased it and added a solarium (with arched windows said to have been built to resemble a railroad observation car) as well as several other additions. The sprawling structure has been converted into offices.

After turning west on Robinson Street, you can see the Governor's Mansion straight ahead and four blocks away, on the corner of Mountain and Robinson streets. Across Robinson from the Yerington home is the former residence of Dr. William Henry Cavell (402 West Robinson), a successful local dentist who built his attractive bungalow in 1907. It is still a private home. Up the street is the William Stewart House (503 West Robinson), erected in 1886 for Senator William Stewart, one of Nevada's first U.S. senators. The house later served as a private hospital and, after 1935, was owned by longtime Nevada state highway engineer Robert A. Allen.

At this point, the trek on Robinson heads right into the heart of Carson City's historic district. To the right is the magnificent Duane L. Bliss Mansion (710 West Robinson), the largest private home in the state when it was built in 1879. Designed in the Victorian Italianate style that was popular at the time, the house has 8,000 square feet of living space, which includes two parlors, six bedrooms, and a ballroom. It was the first residence in Carson City to have gas heating and lighting. Over the years, it has been used as a private residence and a bed-and-breakfast.

Across Robinson from the Bliss place is the Bender House (707 West Robinson), constructed in 1867. Its original owner was George Nourse, Nevada's first attorney general, but it is usually referred to by the name of its second owner, David Bender, a Virginia & Truckee Railroad agent who bought it in 1875. Later, J. T. Davis, a superintendent of the V&T and Carson City's mayor, owned the 3,000-square-foot home. During Davis's ownership, the home gained bay windows and its distinctive round front porch overlooking a vast lawn area. It remains a private residence.

Just ahead is perhaps the capital city's most famous house, the Nevada Governor's Mansion. This two-story Neoclassical home was constructed between 1908 and 1909 at a cost of about $22,700. Previous Nevada governors had either built their own homes in Carson City (many along Mountain Street) or rented living quarters during their terms. According to Robert Nylen, curator of history at the Nevada State Museum, a major reason for the lack of a proper governor's residence during the state's first four decades was "class politics." He has written that while there were several attempts to fund a home for the state's chief executive, many legislators were reluctant to spend public money on such a project because there was a belief that it would create a class barrier between the governor, who would live in such a grand palace, and the general public.

Finally, in 1907, legislators agreed that the governor needed somewhere to live and appropriated $40,000 for building and furnishing a mansion. Reno architect George A. Ferris, who also designed the McKinley Park School in Reno and the former Civic Auditorium in Carson City (now home of the Children's Museum of Northern Nevada), was selected to design the twenty-three-room home, which had a formal dining room, a grand entry, a pair of salons, a private den, a large kitchen, and upstairs bedrooms. In subsequent years, the structure has been renovated several times, most recently in 1999–2000. During that $5 million remodeling, which was privately funded, a 6,608-square-foot addition was built north of the mansion, called the Nevada Room, with a commercial kitchen and meeting space for up to three hundred people.

If you turn south on Mountain Street you enter a row of homes each of which has great historical significance to Carson City. For instance, the brick-and-wood Clapp/Rickey home (512 North Mountain), directly south of the Governor's Mansion, was for many years the home of a prominent banker and rancher, who also served in the Nevada Legislature. The original portion of the home was constructed about 1870 for educators Hannah Clapp and Eliza Babcock. In 1886, the home was sold to former Nevada governor C. C. Stevenson, who died in the house on September 21, 1890. His widow sold the structure, which has been remodeled and expanded over the years, to banker Thomas Rickey and his wife. An interesting side note is that Rickey and his wife sold to the state—for ten dollars—the land on which the Governor's Mansion is built. One legend is that Mrs. Rickey made the donation while her husband was out of town and when he returned he couldn't withdraw the offer because of all the goodwill it had generated. In the early 1950s,

Dick Graves, owner of the Carson Nugget, purchased the house after he moved to Nevada from Idaho.

Adjacent to the Clapp/Rickey house is the Ernest T. Krebs Sr.– Edward Peterson home (500 North Mountain), built in 1914. The first owner, Dr. Krebs, was a well-known local physician and surgeon who made a name for himself by developing a cure for influenza that was based on traditional Washoe Indian remedies. In 1918, he sold the house to Edward Peterson, who worked as an agent for the Virginia & Truckee Railroad for twenty-seven years and served two terms as state controller. The house is one of Carson City's most famous residences because it was featured prominently in the 1976 film *The Shootist,* which was actor John Wayne's final movie. Like the Rickey House, it remains a private residence.

Just down the street is the Marshall Robinson home (406 North Mountain), which was built in 1873. The original owner was one of the founders of the *Carson Daily Appeal* (now the *Nevada Appeal*) newspaper. In 1884, Robinson sold the home to James Raycraft, a member of a pioneer Genoa family and owner of one of the state's first automobile garages. Like the Krebs-Peterson house, the Robinson dwelling was the setting for a movie, *Chicken Every Sunday,* a 1949 screwball comedy starring Dan Dailey, Celeste Holm, and a young Natalie Wood. It continues to be a private home.

Adjacent to the Robinson place is the former home of Governor Reinhold Sadler (310 North Mountain). Although generally referred to as the Sadler House, it was actually built in 1878 by Edward Niles, publisher of another early Carson City newspaper, the *Carson Times.* Sadler acquired it in 1896 (he served as governor from 1896 to 1902) and it was used as the unofficial Governor's Mansion during his term. It also remains a private residence.

Of course, there are many other equally historic residences and buildings scattered throughout the west side and in the rest of the city, such as the Sears-Ferris House, built in 1869, and the childhood home of George Washington Gale Ferris Jr., the inventor of the Ferris wheel (311 West Third), and the Carson Brewing Company (449 West King), a sturdy brick structure erected in 1865 that was used to manufacture "Tahoe Beer" for nearly one hundred years. Later, it served as the offices of the

Nevada Appeal newspaper. Today, the Sears-Ferris house has been converted to offices, while the Carson Brewing building is now the Brewery Arts Center.

Newer structures are proof that Carson City remains a vital, living, growing community rather than some historical artifact with its future dependent on its past. They, too, illustrate the passage of time from blocky, functional but inelegant state office buildings, like the Blasdel Building, erected in the mid-1950s, to the classic but modern Supreme Court Building, completed in 1991.

While buildings may be the most obvious measurement for seeing the changes that have come to Carson City over the past century and a half, they don't tell the community's full story. Fortunately, as the state capital city and one of Nevada's earliest settlements, Carson has been observed and described in numerous historical books, letters, and documents. For example, Chicagoan Caroline M. Churchill described Carson City in July in the early 1870s as a hot, dry, windy place in which "the pigs lie in their mud baths; poodle dogs, that have not been sheared, creep under the sidewalk; the voice of the bird is silent as if listening for the Washoe-zephyr; [and] the perspiring voter freely imbibes his favorite beverage."

Another transplant, Jacob Klein, moved to Carson City from Placerville, California, in 1860 and became a partner in the John Wagner & Company brewery (later known as the Carson Brewing Company). In an 1883 memoir, Klein described the early settlement: "When I came here in 1860 . . . there was nothing in Carson only a few houses, perhaps 30 or 40 houses." Nellie Mighels Davis, who arrived in the capital city in 1865, later recalled arriving in the community on a stagecoach from California. In an interview she said, "My first sight of Carson made me think of a little toy village, with its tiny one-story houses and its few trees. Looking down, it appeared to me like a doll town and I wondered at the time why the houses were built so small and squat, but I afterward learned that the houses [were] made only one story high on account of strong winds . . . humorously christened 'Washoe Zephyrs.'"

Since then, Carson City has grown and evolved, largely because of its place as the seat of Nevada state government. While perhaps indulging in a bit of hyperbole, Reno writer Deke Castleman once wrote that the community is the *power* center, to which all the state looks for vision, direction, leadership, and order. . . . [T]his calm, comfortable, pretty, and friendly town seems to reside atop a rare locus of *planetary* power. These emanations from the Earth certainly infused its founders and partisans with a special zeal and authority. And they continue to infuse an elite corps of residents and visitors, who appreciate the city's excellent size, central location, friendliness, fascinating facilities, and subtle sensation of powerful forces still at play just below the surface of this capital of the most unusual state in the country.

Perhaps the last word when it comes to defining Carson City should belong to writer Robert Laxalt, who grew up in the capital city during the 1930s and '40s. In his book *Travels with My Royal,* Laxalt described Carson City as "a polite town. From the time I was a young boy, I said hello to everyone I met on Main Street and they said hello to me. Nobody said I had to. It was the accepted thing to do, from the governor on down to the town drunk who swamped out the whorehouses just off Main Street."

So, in addition to being the state capital, Carson City is the center of the universe and a polite town. That's not something that can be said about every community.

Chapter One

Becoming Abe Curry's Town

Now, therefore, be it known, that I, Abraham Lincoln, President of the United States, in accordance with the duty imposed upon me by the Act of Congress aforesaid, do hereby declare and proclaim that the said State of Nevada is admitted into the Union on an equal footing with the original states.

In witness whereof, I have hereunder set my hand, and caused the seal of the United States to be affixed.

Done at the city of Washington this thirty-first day of October, in the year of our Lord one thousand eight hundred and sixty-four, and of the independence of the United States the eighty-ninth.

—ABRAHAM LINCOLN *(October 31, 1864)*

Carson City founders Abraham Curry, John J. Musser, and Francis M. Proctor (later joined by Benjamin F. Green, Proctor's father-in-law, who became a minor partner) would undoubtedly be proud of what has become of their little settlement. It is unlikely they could have foreseen the sprawling campus of state government buildings, the rows of houses lined up like dominoes, or the complex grid of paved streets and highways that would eventually cover the acres of sagebrush, greasewood, and grassland that they purchased in August of 1858.

However, the three weren't the first to set eyes on the Eagle Valley area in which Carson City is located. The Washoes were there much earlier; the valley served as a wintering place for many centuries. The tribe would head to Lake Tahoe in the summer, where they could find abundant fish and game, then move to the lower elevations of the eastern slope of the Sierra Nevada during the colder months. A dirt road that leads between Carson City and Lake Tahoe—now known as King's

Canyon Road—is believed to originally have been a traditional trail for the Washoes to travel between the two places. In the 1850s, fortune seekers from California used the path to travel to Virginia City, after fabulously rich silver deposits had been discovered there. In 1863, it became a toll road between Carson City and Lake Tahoe and in the early twentieth century the route was incorporated into the transcontinental Lincoln Highway. In recent decades, it has been largely abandoned and is slowly returning to its original state as a walking trail.

Eagle Valley was not the first place settled in the land that became Nevada. In 1850, a handful of prospectors had begun placer mining in the Gold Canyon area, above present-day Dayton, and a group of Mormons (members of the Church of Jesus Christ of Latter-day Saints), led by Captain Joseph DeMont, established a crude trading post in the Carson Valley (near present-day Genoa). The post, which became known as Mormon Station, supplied emigrant wagon trains and groups heading to California with provisions and goods. At the end of the summer, DeMont and his companions, including Hampton S. Beatie and Abner Blackburn, sold the business to a California trader and relocated to Salt Lake City.

In her book, *Devils Will Reign,* historian Sally Zanjani speculated that Beatie probably told Colonel John Reese, a Mormon for whom Beatie worked as a store clerk, about the success of the trading post. Intrigued, Reese and a small group set out from Salt Lake City in May 1851 with thirteen wagons carrying supplies, food, seeds, farm equipment, and other goods. A month later, he arrived in the Carson Valley and put down roots. According to Zanjani, Reese was astounded by how much money he made selling his crops—primarily turnips—to the emigrants and nearby miners and soon added other services, including a blacksmith shop.

Eagle Valley Pioneers

In late 1851, after unsuccessfully placer mining in Gold Canyon, Joseph Barnard, Frank Barnard, Frank Hall, W. L. Hall, A. J. Rollins, and George Follensbye staked a claim on land in the valley north of Carson Valley and established a trading post and ranch. They named the area Eagle Valley (and the post Eagle Station), after Frank Hall shot and killed an eagle, which he stuffed and mounted over the trading post's doorway. The station, believed to have been located near the present-day site of Fifth and Thompson streets in Carson City, was the first permanent settlement in the valley and was also known as the Eagle Ranch. The owners planted crops and grew hay, which they sold to travelers heading to California.

While records are sketchy, other early Eagle Valley pioneers included Dr. Benjamin L. King, who established a small resort in the valley in 1852 (a canyon to the west of the valley bears his name), and Jacob Rose, who built a house to the north (Rose Canyon is named after him) and owned land in Washoe Valley.

In 1854, according to Thompson & West's *History of Nevada 1881,* the Barnard brothers, the Halls, Rollins, and Follensbye sold their holdings (which included the trading post and ranch) to Colonel Reese and E. L. Barnard (evidently no relation to the Barnard brothers), who, in turn, sold it to several Mormon families. Three years later, Mormon leader Brigham Young called the members of his congregation to Salt Lake City to defend the city against an approaching military force sent by President James Buchanan to confront the Mormons and re-affirm federal jurisdiction over the region. (The conflict ended peacefully for the most part in July 1858 when Young agreed to step down as the territorial governor and accept federal oversight.)

As the Mormon settlers hastily prepared to head to Utah, they were forced to sell their ranches and equipment at bargain prices to the remaining non-Mormons (referred to as "Gentiles" by church members). In some cases, it has been reported that Mormon property was simply taken over by the non-Mormons, who refused to pay anything for the land and other valuables left behind. In 1856, Mormon elder Orson Hyde, a prominent leader in Genoa (he named the community) who was returning to Salt Lake City, leased plots of land and a new sawmill he and several partners had completed in Washoe Valley to Jacob Rose and R. D. Sides for $10,000. He reported receiving mules, a worn harness, two yokes of oxen, and a wagon as an advance on the payment. However, after Hyde's departure, Rose and Sides apparently felt little obligation to pay the debt.

In 1862, an angry Hyde fired off a letter, now known as Orson Hyde's Curse, that demanded immediate payment of $20,000 (what he estimated the property was worth) and threatened that if he was not properly compensated, "You shall be visited of the Lord of Hosts with thunder and with earthquakes and with floods, with pestilence and with famine until your names are not known amongst men."

With the departure of the Mormons, much of Eagle Valley fell into the hands of John Bracken Mankins, a man described in Thompson & West as "an old pirate, mountaineer and frontiersman" who was "a rough, passionate, illiterate fellow; given to quarreling with his neighbors." Mankins reportedly acquired the Mormon holdings for very little money and gained ownership of a large portion of the valley, which, by mid-1858, still had only a handful of residents, including Mankins and his family (four daughters and an adopted Indian boy), Dr. King and his family, the Jacob Rose family, the Mark Stebbins family, and the Samuel Nevers family.

Governing Utah Territory

The Latter-day Saints (Mormons) arrived in the valley of the Great Salt Lake in July 1847. As a result of religious persecution, members of the religion had been forced to leave Nauvoo, Illinois, in 1846. An advance party of 143 men and women, led by church leader Brigham Young, arrived in the Salt Lake Valley (1,040 miles from Illinois), on the western front of the Wasatch Range, and began setting up a community for the faithful. The Utah Territory, with Brigham Young as the territorial governor, was created as part of the Compromise of 1850 (legislation designed to resolve territorial disputes and balance the interests of the slave-holding states and those that opposed slavery). The original boundaries of the territory encompassed all of present-day Utah as well as much of Nevada and small portions of Colorado and Wyoming.

Given the enormous size of the territory, it was no surprise that territorial authorities gave little thought to establishing any type of government in what is now western Nevada. In November 1851, a provisional government was organized at Mormon Station in Carson Valley, which, according to *The Political History of Nevada* (1996), was an indication that residents either "ignored the fact that they were subject to the laws of the Territory of Utah or they considered those laws inadequate." The settlers' government, which conducted six public meetings between

November 1851 and August 1854, declared that its goal was to protect individual property rights as well as create a law enforcement and court system. They also crafted a petition to Congress requesting to be separated from the Utah Territory.

As more people settled into the western portion of Utah Territory, primarily the Carson Valley, it became increasingly difficult for the provisional government to accommodate their needs. There was also continued tension between Mormon and non-Mormon residents. Some began to promote annexation to the adjacent state of California while others pushed for a new territory. In response, Utah's territorial legislature created Carson County in 1854; it was an attempt to establish a more formal government for the region and, it was widely believed, to maintain Mormon control of the area. The jurisdiction extended over more than twenty thousand square miles and included today's Carson City as well as Douglas, Lyon, and Storey counties, along with large portions of Washoe, Pershing, Mineral, and Churchill counties and pieces of Nye and Esmeralda counties. Mormon Station (renamed Genoa in 1855) was designated the county seat.

Territorial officials, however, did not immediately organize Carson County or send representatives, so once again there was talk of setting up an alternative form of government. Finally, in 1855, U.S. District Court judge George P. Stiles was named to preside over legal matters in Carson County, and Orson Hyde, one of the twelve apostles of the Mormon church (the church's primary governing council), was appointed probate judge. The two men, who arrived in Genoa in June, were tasked with setting up the county government.

Hyde held elections on September 20 to fill the county offices. According to Sally Zanjani, "All the Mormon candidates [Hyde] chose won, confirming the settlers' fears of Mormon domination." The election did little to resolve the simmering ill will between the two groups. One Carson Valley resident, Thomas Knott, had so little regard for the Mormons that when his son, Elzy, was killed by a Mormon during an argument over a saddle, Thomas Knott refused to bury the young man in the town cemetery because it contained deceased Mormons. He laid him to rest in his own backyard instead.

Throughout the following year, additional members of the Latter-day

Saints arrived in Carson Valley and Eagle Valley. During elections in August 1856, Mormons had clearly become the majority and swept all county offices except one (assessor-treasurer). In early 1857, in response to the difficulty in maintaining jurisdiction over Carson County because it was so far away, the Utah Territorial Legislature voted to attach remote Carson County to Great Salt Lake County. All court and county records were moved to Salt Lake City, which was some five hundred miles away. This effectively left the region without a functioning local government.

In mid-1857, however, the Mormon era came to an abrupt end when Brigham Young called his followers back to Salt Lake City to prepare for conflict with the advancing federal army. According to *The Political History of Nevada* (1996), the "departure of the Mormons resulted in the almost complete depopulation of the Truckee Meadows and Washoe and Eagle valleys."

With the exodus of the Mormons from the eastern Sierra, the region was once again largely on its own when it came to legal matters and law enforcement. Major William Ormsby, a relative newcomer who had arrived in Genoa in the spring of 1857, immediately saw the possibilities for political and financial gain. Ormsby, along with his friend Judge James Crane, another recent arrival, began to promote the creation of a new territory, carved from the Utah Territory. Ormsby, who was born in Pennsylvania, had previously participated in adventurer William Walker's ill-fated attempt in 1856 to lead a small army of expansion-minded Americans in a takeover of Nicaragua (and then seek to have his conquered territory, along with several other South American countries, admitted into the Union as slave-holding states). After that effort failed, Ormsby relocated to Genoa to seek his fame and fortune. For several months while living there, he and his wife took care of two of the daughters of the Paiute Chief Winnemucca. One of the daughters, Sarah, later wrote a book about her people's plight; it was the first book ever written by a Native American woman.

Ormsby and Crane quickly became leaders of the effort to create a new territory from the lands of the far western Utah Territory. In April 1857, Ormsby organized a petition

Major William Ormsby, ca. 1855. (Nevada State Archives)

addressed to President James Buchanan requesting the creation of a separate territory. The initiative was endorsed by California's governor and state legislature, and signed by Ormsby on behalf of local residents. In August 1857, Crane was elected to represent the group in Washington, D.C. According to Sally Zanjani, Ormsby and Crane's efforts fizzled after the conflict between the federal government and the Mormons was resolved in mid-1858. Congress moved on to other issues and the importance of creating a new, non-Mormon territory on the eastern slope of the Sierra faded for at least a little while.

Curry, Green, Musser, and Proctor, Inc.

Sometime in 1855, Ohio businessman Abraham "Abe" Curry and his eighteen-year-old son, Charles, arrived in San Francisco to, like so many others, seek their fortunes in California. During the next two years, Curry and his son ran a variety of businesses in northern California mining camps, including a bowling alley in the mining camp of Red Dog. In 1857, Curry and his son traveled to Downieville, where rich ore had been discovered. There, they invested in real estate and worked as building contractors. While living in Downieville, Abe Curry became friends with Benjamin F. Green, John J. Musser, and Francis "Frank" M. Proctor. According to Curry's biographer, Doris Cerveri, Green was a

Abe Curry, ca. 1870. (Nevada Historical Society)

partner in a jewelry and watchmaking shop, and served as Sierra County treasurer in 1857, while Proctor was an attorney, active in local politics and married to Green's daughter. Musser was also a lawyer and had served as district attorney of Sierra County in 1856–57.

In the spring of 1858, Abe and Charles Curry, Musser, and Proctor, as well as Frank Green, brother of Benjamin, and two friends, W. B. Hickock and Captain William T. Ferguson, journeyed into western Utah Territory to determine its investment potential. Cerveri reported that the group visited Steamboat Hot Springs, Washoe Lake, Franktown, and Genoa, becoming convinced of the region's possibilities before returning to Downieville.

In July 1858, the two Currys, Frank and Benjamin Green, Musser, and Proctor headed by stagecoach to Genoa, intending to purchase land to build a store. While there are no records of what happened, popular legend has it that Curry offered $1,000 for a corner lot in Genoa but was turned down by the owners. Unable to find anything else suitable for their plans, the group traveled north to Eagle Valley. The area was not as desirable as the green, grassy Carson Valley because its natural vegetation had been overgrazed by the dozens of wagon trains that had passed through on their way to California. Curry and his partners most likely found a valley that consisted of dry, dusty flats interspersed with clumps of sagebrush and desert grasses.

The group approached John Mankins, owner of much of the land in the valley, and offered to purchase his holdings. According to former Nevada state archivist Guy Louis Rocha, who has examined the original deed, on August 12, 1858, Mankins sold about 865 acres plus a separate one-half section claimed and taken up by George Mankins (John's brother) to Curry, Proctor, and Musser for $1,000, for a down payment of $300 and the balance to be paid within thirty days. Benjamin Green witnessed the transaction and, reportedly, was later given half of his son-in-law's (Proctor's) one-third share. Members of the Mankins family still live in Carson City and there is a John Mankins Park at 3051 Oak Ridge Drive in Carson City.

The Curry-Musser-Proctor group hired John F. Long of the nearby community of Chinatown (now called Dayton) to survey and lay out, or plat, a town site. According to Cerveri, Long didn't think much of the site and told Curry and his group to sell and look for a place that had more potential. Cerveri wrote that Curry also offered to give Long property in Eagle Valley in lieu of his fee for the survey. Long allegedly rejected the deal, saying he would rather have Curry owe him money than give him a worthless piece of ground. After the acreage was platted, the four partners divided the town lots amongst themselves. Lots were also offered to anyone who promised to build on them, with payment based on ability to pay. In this way, the group was able to immediately gain residents for the new community. Frank Proctor is credited with naming the community after the Carson River, which flows through the south end of the valley. The river, in turn, was named in honor of explorer Christopher "Kit" Carson, who had served as a scout for John C. Frémont during his expedition through Nevada and the West in 1843–44. In 1864, during the

The corner of Second and Carson streets, including the original Ormsby House (*center*) in 1863. (Nevada State Archives)

second Nevada State Constitutional Convention, Proctor, who was a delegate, declared, "I named the city myself. Carson City is what we used to call it."

Among those who purchased lots was Major William Ormsby of Genoa, who soon opened a general merchandise store—thought to be one of Carson City's first commercial businesses—and built a two-story house/hotel. Doris Cerveri wrote that the politically ambitious Ormsby planned to use the upper rooms of his hotel as meeting space for the territorial legislature. On November 18, 1858, a federal post office was formally established in Carson City (John F. Long, the man who had surveyed the town, was named postmaster).

Certainly aware of all of the talk about creating a new territory, Curry set aside a four-acre portion of land in the center of the planned community for a public square or possible territorial capitol. Streets were named for the three main partners, Curry, Musser, and Proctor. Curry immediately set to work constructing buildings for the new community. About two miles east of the center of town, Curry and his partners found a large sandstone outcropping and a natural warm springs. Musser and Proctor didn't see the potential of either and gave Curry their interests, while Green reportedly sold his share for twenty-two pounds of butter and a pony. Curry began quarrying stone at the site and dammed up the springs for a small public bathhouse. In 1861, he built the two-story Warm Springs Hotel. While Curry was busy constructing homes and other buildings, Musser and Proctor opened law offices and Green opened a jewelry and gunsmithing business.

Location, Location, Location

The news of the discovery of rich silver deposits in Gold Canyon (between present-day Virginia City and Dayton) in the spring of 1859 generated plenty of excitement and activity in Carson City. As fortune seekers flocked to the area, they passed through the newly minted community of Carson City, often stopping to stock up on supplies and other goods. In 1860, writer and artist J. Ross Browne was among the first journalists to visit the future Comstock Lode (the name eventually given to the main silver vein in Virginia City). Browne passed through Carson City, which he estimated had a population of 1,200 to 1,500. In *A Peep at Washoe,* his collection of observations and drawings, Browne gave it a mixed review, describing it as "really quite a pretty and thrifty little town" but also noting that land speculation was rampant in the town because of rumors that Carson City was going to be designated as the new seat of government.

After visiting both communities, Browne succinctly and candidly recounted the major differences between Virginia City and Carson City, which he said had already become rivals:

Virginia City—a mud-hole; climate, hurricanes and snow; water, a dilution of arsenic, plumbago, and copperas; wood, none at all except sage-brush; no title to property, and no property worth having.

Carson City—a mere accident; occupation of the inhabitants, waylaying strangers bound for Virginia; business, selling whiskey, and so dull at that, men fall asleep in the middle of the street going from one grogery to another; productions, grass and weeds on the Plaza.

Virginia City's mining boom forever changed Carson City. Once a kind of sleepy backwater town that survived off travelers heading to California as well as small-scale ranching and agriculture, it quickly evolved into a kind of suburb of Virginia City, its economy dependent on miners and on land and mining stock speculation. Mining fever seemed

to spread to everyone, including Abe Curry. In May 1859, Curry, his son, and several friends invested in a claim that became known as the Gould and Curry Mine. About six months later, Curry sold his share for a reported $2,000 in order to have enough money to send for his wife and family, who were living in Ohio. The mine eventually earned several million dollars.

Former state archivist Guy Louis Rocha noted, "Times were booming in Carson City by the end of 1859 with the gold and silver discoveries on the nearby Comstock."

Hank Monk: "Keep Your Seat, Horace"

One of the most famous men to live in Nevada in the nineteenth century was stagecoach driver Hank Monk. Born in 1826, Monk began driving a stage between Genoa and Placerville, California, in about 1857. For the next several decades, Monk gained a reputation for speed—it was said he could make the eighty-seven-mile journey faster than any other stage driver. In July 1859, renowned New York newspaper editor and social reformer Horace Greeley hired Monk to quickly transport him from Carson Valley to Placerville, where Greeley was scheduled to speak. Greeley was concerned about arriving late, so he asked the driver if he could make certain the stage reached its destination by 5 PM that evening. Hank is said to have promised he would get him there in time. Greeley later wrote that Monk took off at a "breakneck rate" that bounced him all over the coach and raised such a cloud of dust that it was difficult to see. Monk later told a writer that during the ride he looked inside to make sure that Greeley was doing fine and saw the bald-headed editor bouncing all over the coach, trying in vain to hang on to anything he could grab. According to Monk's account, at one point Greeley shouted to Monk that the driver could slow a little because he didn't mind if they arrived an hour or two late. Monk said he told Greeley, "Horace, keep your seat! I told you I would get you there by five o'clock, and by God I'll do it, if the axles hold!"

True to his word, Monk delivered Greeley on time to a reception committee that was waiting a dozen miles east of Placerville. Shortly thereafter, Greeley wrote his account of the terrifying ride over the Sierra Nevada. The story made Monk a national celebrity and the driver, who moved from Placerville to Carson City in the early 1860s, enjoyed telling it to anyone who would listen. One of those who heard the tale was a young Mark Twain, who incorporated an exaggerated version into both his western lecture tour of 1866 and his 1872 book, *Roughing It*. In both his lectures and his book, Twain would repeat the story three times for emphasis in order to show how tedious it had become from being told so often.

As a result of Twain's comedic telling of the story, Hank Monk was immortalized as one of Nevada's premier stagecoach drivers. In 1879, Monk was the stage driver for former president Ulysses S. Grant, when he traveled via Clear Creek Canyon from Spooner Summit to Carson City. In 1880, when President Rutherford B. Hayes visited northern Nevada (the first sitting president to do so), he specifically requested that Monk serve as his driver on the ten-mile stage ride from Carson City to Spooner Summit above Lake Tahoe. According to accounts, President Hayes asked Monk if he could get him to his destination on time and the

Stage driver Hank Monk became so well known that in 1878 Carson City composer John P. Meder wrote dance music in his honor, the "Hank Monk Schottische." (Special Collections, University of Nevada, Reno Libraries)

driver repeated what he said to Greeley—to sit down and he would get him there in time.

Monk continued to drive stages between Carson City and Placerville until his death in 1883. He is buried in the Lone Mountain Cemetery in Carson City.

Planting the Seeds

The rapid growth of Carson City and Virginia City, as well as the resulting problems regarding disputed property and mineral rights and crime, made it apparent that there was a serious need for some type of law and order in the far western Utah Territory. In June 1859, local residents gathered in Carson City to discuss whether to reopen the question of seeking territorial status for the region. The consensus was to move ahead with a provisional government and a month later a constitutional convention was held in Genoa. There, delegates voted once again to have James Crane represent their interests in Washington, D.C., and elected John J. Musser as convention president. Isaac Roop of Susanville (at the time, that part of eastern California was thought to be part of the new territory) was selected to be governor of the Nevada Territory. Crane died suddenly just before he was to leave for Washington and was replaced by Musser, who departed for the nation's capital in December 1859.

While Musser was unsuccessful in getting Congress to act immediately, the issue gained support throughout 1860 as the true nature of the Comstock Lode's wealth became known and the region's population began to explode. Additionally, Congress was made aware of the generally chaotic political conditions—appointed Utah Territory officials, the provisional (but unrecognized) territorial government led by Roop, and federal officials all claimed jurisdiction over the region.

And, after the events of May 12, 1860, it seemed that residents of the eastern Sierra might also have need of some federal protection.

The Pyramid Lake War of 1860

Relations grew strained between the Native Americans of Nevada and the rapidly increasing numbers of white settlers in the region. The Washoe (also spelled Washo) and the more numerous Paiute people that lived in the eastern Sierra were nomadic, moving from place to place and living off the land. The settlers, however, erected wooden and brick structures, put up fences, and chopped down trees, including the essential piñon pine. The Native Americans harvested pine nuts from those trees, providing a food source for the tribe during the colder months when gathering and hunting were limited. In *Sand in a Whirlwind: The Paiute Indian War of 1860,* author Ferol Egan wrote that the newcomers "began to cut more and more piñon pine for firewood. Never once did they think that they were destroying the pine nut orchards of the Paiutes and Washos." Despite the tension, the Washoe and Paiute groups resisted open conflict with the whites, recognizing that their superior weapons and numbers would eventually overwhelm the tribes.

In the spring of 1860, however, a series of events exacerbated the situation, resulting in what have been called the Battles of Pyramid Lake

Chief Winnemucca, ca. 1880.
(Nevada Historical Society)

.

(May 12 and June 2). The main cause of the war was the kidnapping and molesting of two Paiute girls, both believed to have been about twelve years old, by the three Williams brothers, owners of Williams Station, a crude trading post located south of Pyramid Lake, along the Carson River. Richard "Tennessee" Allen, a Genoa-based correspondent for the *San Francisco Herald,* wrote that Williams Station was similar to the many disreputable "little grog shops" along the emigrant trail and opined "scarcely one of whom is too good to commit the worst of crimes."

According to several reports, in early May 1860, the girls were out digging for roots when they were captured by the Williamses and held captive at the station. The parents of the two young women followed their trail to the station but could not find them there and were assured by the owners that the girls had not been in the area. A few days later, a Paiute stopped at the station to trade and heard the girls' voices coming from a cellar. He immediately told the parents, who quickly returned with a small, armed group of Paiutes and Bannocks that included Natchez, brother of Sarah Winnemucca. Upon finding the girls, the party killed two of the Williams brothers as well as three white men who were also in the station at the time. They burned the station and rescued the girls.

The third Williams brother, James, had been camping away from the station at the time of the attack. He returned to find the burned structures and the dead bodies. He rode to Virginia City and spread the word that the Paiutes were massacring settlers—and claimed more than five hundred Paiute warriors had been chasing him. Not surprisingly, the residents of Virginia City, Carson City, and Genoa were fearful and outraged. Some packed up and headed for California while others began to prepare for war. Despite the fact that the raiding party had struck only Williams Station and had not attacked any other locations, many proclaimed that the Indians had launched a full-out assault against the settlers.

Sally Zanjani has noted that foremost among those wanting to wage war against the Paiutes was William Ormsby. She speculates that the ambitious Ormsby, who, ironically, had allowed Chief Winnemucca's daughters to live with his family for several months, saw a quick victory as a surefire way to make him a political force in the future Nevada Territory. He gathered together a local militia, the Carson Rangers, and joined the disorganized citizen army that had coalesced to hunt down the Paiutes and teach them a lesson. While more than one hundred armed men had joined up, the group had no leader, as the militias of each community refused to follow orders from anyone other than their own commanders.

The group traveled to Williams Station, where they buried the dead, then headed to Pyramid Lake. Because no one was in command, the various militias did not ride in a tight formation but were strung out along the trail. On the afternoon of May 12, the first group of militia riders spotted a handful of Indians at the mouth of a bowl-shaped meadow five miles south of Pyramid Lake. About thirty men raced into the meadow after the Indians, but as they closed a larger group of Indians began firing at them from both sides. They apparently attempted to retreat but the ground was muddy, which hampered their movements. Almost simultaneously, another group of warriors had circled to the south of the main body of the militia, effectively cutting off any possibility of escape.

For the next two hours, the militia members found themselves mired in a muddy gulch, fighting in all directions. When the battle was finally over, about 75 of the 105 militia members were dead, including William Ormsby. While difficult to measure, it is believed that casualties among the Indians were light.

Following the disastrous encounter, the federal government assembled a more formidable army of 207 trained soldiers and 544 volunteers to march on Pyramid Lake. On June 2, this more disciplined force returned to the scene of the first battle and once again engaged the Paiutes. This time the results were different, with the Paiutes eventually fleeing north into the Black Rock Desert. Following the second battle, the military established a temporary encampment south of Pyramid Lake and erected two posts in Nevada, at Fort Churchill, not far from the former site of Williams Station, and Camp McDermit on the Oregon border.

Birthing Nevada

In the months following the battles at Pyramid Lake, conditions for the creation of a Nevada Territory gradually improved. According to Sally Zanjani, the Republicans in Congress made a concerted effort to create more free (non-slavery) territories in the West, particularly as the Southern states prepared to secede from the Union. In February 1861, legislation was introduced to create the Nevada, Dakota, and Colorado territories. On March 2, 1861, two days before President Abraham Lincoln assumed office, outgoing President James Buchanan signed the enabling bill into law.

In addition to setting out the boundaries of the new territory, which was carved from the Utah Territory, the legislation specified territorial officers, including a governor, secretary, chief justice, and attorney general. James W. Nye, a former New York City police commissioner and Lincoln loyalist, was named territorial governor, while Orion Clemens of Missouri, who had apprenticed in the law office of Edward Bates (who later became President Lincoln's attorney general), was chosen as secretary of the territory (with some duties similar to a lieutenant governor). Joining Clemens in Nevada was his younger brother, Samuel.

The creation of the Nevada Territory was a defining moment in Carson City's history. One of Governor Nye's first acts was to hold elections for territorial legislators, and then he ordered them to convene in Carson City on October 1, 1861, to begin creating laws for the new territory. Doris Cerveri notes that when the legislators were unable to find a suitable location for their first session, Abraham Curry, who had been elected as a territorial representative, offered use of his Warm Springs Hotel (including transportation to and from the hotel) at no cost. One of the early bills that passed the Nevada Territorial Legislature was one that designated Carson City as the seat of the new territory. Additionally, the legislature created nine counties: Churchill, Douglas, Esmeralda, Humboldt, Lake (later renamed Roop and, in 1883, consolidated with Washoe), Lyon, Storey, Washoe, and Ormsby. The

Governor James Nye, ca. 1870s. (Library of Congress)

last included Carson City and was named to honor the fallen William Ormsby.

The territorial legislature met in Carson City three times between 1861 and 1864. By 1861, Curry had completed the Great Basin Hotel, an impressive stone structure in the center of Carson City, which hosted the second and third sessions of the legislature as well as the two constitutional conventions. (In 1862, Curry sold the hotel to Ormsby County, which converted it into county offices and rented space to the territory for the legislature and state supreme court.) The site of the hotel, the southwest corner of Musser and Carson streets, is the location of the historic Neoclassical Ormsby County Courthouse, which was completed in 1922 and is currently part of the Nevada attorney general office complex.

Eager to gain statehood, territorial officials held an election on September 2, 1863, to gauge support for the concept, which was approved by a substantial margin of 6,660 votes to 1,502 votes. That was followed by the First Constitutional Convention, which began on November 2, to draft a state constitution. While the effort was not sanctioned by Congress, it was believed that having a constitution would help streamline the process of becoming a state. The convention produced a document largely based on those adopted in New York and California. The final product, however, was controversial because it allowed for the taxation of mines regardless of whether they were productive. As a result, on January 19, 1864, voters (most of whom worked in the mining industry, then in a recession) rejected the initial constitution by a more than 4-to-1 majority.

Meanwhile, Congress continued deliberating the question of allowing Nevada and several other territories to become states. *The Political History of Nevada* points out that "Nevada's statehood bill was part of a national plan to secure more Republican votes for President Lincoln's reelection." Several statehood bills were introduced in 1863 and 1864 before one finally passed both houses. On March 21, 1864, President Lincoln signed the enabling act. The new law required Nevada to adopt a constitution that included certain provisions stipulated by Congress and mandated presidential review and approval.

The Second Constitutional Convention was quickly called together in July to write a more acceptable constitution. The second convention adopted the provisions of the enabling act, which included the outlawing of slavery in Nevada and a statement that all undistributed public lands would be retained by the federal government, and the taxation language that had been opposed by the mining industry was revised. This version was approved on September 7, 1864, by a vote of 10,375 to 1,184. The final constitution was sent to Washington, D.C., via telegraph at a cost of $3,416.77—the longest and most expensive telegram ever sent at that time. On October 31, 1864, President Lincoln signed a proclamation declaring Nevada statehood. Not surprisingly, when the national elections were held eight days later, Nevadans voted overwhelmingly for the Republican ticket.

The constitution contained a simple provision that was particularly important to the development of Carson City: "The seat of Government shall be at Carson City." Interestingly, the clause also noted that "no appropriation for the erection or purchase of Capitol buildings shall be made during the next three years," which allowed legislators a little time to decide if they wanted to move the state capital to another community. Fortunately for Carson City, it was an action that was never taken.

Of course, that doesn't mean there weren't attempts to take the state capital from Carson City. Even in the first legislative sessions, legislators from other parts of the state tried to persuade their colleagues to consider other options. Much of the opposition to authorizing funds to build a capitol in Carson City came from Lander County officials, who thought booming Austin might be a better site. Lander's state senator D. W. Welty went so far as to describe Carson City as "a swamp" and a "mud hole."

Virginia City also made a few half-hearted tries at snagging the capital. *Territorial Enterprise* owner Joseph Goodman once wrote—tongue in cheek—of an 1864 attempt to claim the capital for Virginia City:

> It is easy enough to obey a gypsy impulse to go anywhere or everywhere, but when you have arrived at your destination without any purpose a feeling of stultification is liable to confront you and ask what it all means. And so, when we deployed ourselves in the blaze of the capital, and anxious denizens inquired what this sudden irruption of the dignitaries of Virginia City signified, we were confounded and unable to reply satisfactorily. But their insistence speedily begot

a purpose. The capital could not be permanently fixed under the Territorial act; its location was at the will of the Legislature, and we determined to remove it to Virginia City.

Goodman counted heads and found that while the assembly would go along with the move, there was a tie vote in the senate. He decided to focus his attention on persuading "Uncle Abe Curry" to switch his vote in favor of Virginia City but was, in turn, convinced to drop his effort by a tearful Curry. "The jig was up, I honored the old man's sentiment, though it swept away our brilliant dream of empire," he concluded.

In 1908, former U.S. senator William M. Stewart of Nevada, who served from 1864 to 1875 and again from 1887 to 1905, reminisced that

Senator William M. Stewart, ca. 1875. (Special Collections, University of Nevada, Reno Libraries)

a committee inquired of me the morning before the election where I thought the capital ought to be, and I told them by all means at Carson, where the climate was excellent, the water good, which would make it a permanent town; whereas Virginia City was a min- ing town and not a suitable place for the capital. They did not disclose the purpose of asking me this question. I remained in Virginia City until after the election, and when the votes were counted I had more than two-thirds of them. There was nothing for me to do but to serve. Knowing that I had been elected for the purpose of locating the capi- tal at Carson, I remained at home during the time the members of the Legislature were coming in from different parts of the Territory. I inquired of each how he wanted his county bounded and where he wanted the county-seat. Each one told me, and I framed a bill divid- ing the Territory into counties and making Carson the capital.

Mark Twain in Carson City

Samuel Langhorne Clemens arrived in Carson City in August 1861. He had traveled by stagecoach to the future Nevada state capital from St. Joseph, Missouri, with his older brother, Orion, who had been appointed territorial secretary by President Abraham Lincoln. The younger

Clemens's plan was to work for his brother, who was assisting the new territorial governor, James Nye, to put in place the structure of a territorial government. Unfortunately, there was no funding for a "secretary to the secretary," so he began casting about for other work.

For the next year, Sam Clemens wandered about the western Nevada–eastern California region. He spent some time at Lake Tahoe and in the mining camps of Unionville (between Lovelock and Winnemucca) and Aurora. While living in Aurora, Clemens began writing humorous articles in the form of letters, which he submitted using a pen name, "Josh," to the *Territorial Enterprise* newspaper in Virginia City. After printing the missives for several months, the paper offered Clemens a position in Virginia City. In a July 30, 1862, letter to his brother, Clemens writes that William H. Barstow, a business manager at the *Enterprise,* had offered him "the post of local reporter for the Enterprise at $25 a week."

Clemens accepted the offer, and began working at the *Enterprise* in September 1862. According to Guy Louis Rocha, Clemens's first major assignment was covering the second territorial legislature, which met at Abe Curry's Great Basin Hotel in Carson City. From November to December 1862, Clemens largely resided in Carson City covering the deliberations of the territorial legislature. Assigning Sam Clemens to cover the legislature was a canny move on the part of the *Enterprise* since he was familiar with many of the main political players as a result of his brother's position in the government.

Interestingly, on January 31, 1863, Sam Clemens wrote a letter from Carson City (his news reports were often filed in the form of letters) to the *Enterprise* and signed it "Mark Twain." It is the first known time that Clemens used his famous pen name in print.

Clemens's next significant mention of the Carson City area occurred on October 28, 1863, when he wrote one of his most infamous articles, "A Bloody Massacre Near Carson." The story, which gained considerable notoriety because of its gory descriptions, tells of a man named Philip Hopkins, who lived with his wife and nine children in a log cabin near Empire City (four miles east of Carson City). According to the article, distraught at having lost all his money in a water company stock fraud, Hopkins slaughtered his wife and seven of his children before slitting his own throat. The horrendous tale generated such an outcry that the next

day Clemens was compelled to file a response. His follow-up message simply read: "I TAKE IT ALL BACK."

Twain biographer Albert Bigelow Paine has written that the story was intended as a hoax but, unfortunately, many people took it seriously. Paine noted that Twain was actually trying to satirize a San Francisco newspaper, which is mentioned disparagingly in the article, for its critical reports about Nevada's mining stocks. Additionally, Twain wanted to poke fun at a California water company that had also recently committed a stock fraud.

A month later, Clemens was back in Carson City covering the events of the First Constitutional Convention. He wrote regular reports to the *Enterprise* about the proceedings throughout most of the two-month session and then, from January to February 1864, reported on the third session of the territorial legislature in Carson City. Throughout the time, he often stayed with his brother Orion, who built a two-story home in Carson City (still standing on the corner of Division and Spear streets) in early 1864.

Following both the First Constitutional Convention and the third territorial legislative session, Clemens participated with a loose-knit group of journalists, observers, and others, known as the "Third House," to lampoon the most recent legislative gatherings. The tradition had apparently started following the territorial legislative sessions in 1861 and 1862.

During the December 1863 meeting of the "Third House," Clemens was chosen president of the convention and, with mock sincerity, said, "This is the proudest moment of my life. I shall always think so. I think so still. I shall ponder over it with unspeakable emotion down to the latest syllable of recorded time."

As a natural storyteller—and during a time when public lecturers were popular attractions—Clemens chose Carson City to try out his public speaking ability. On January 27, 1864, he gave his first paid public lecture as a benefit for the First Presbyterian Church, at which his brother was a prominent member. Clemens reportedly raised more than $200 for the church.

On February 1, 1864, Clemens's eight-year-old niece, Jennie (the only daughter of Orion and Mary "Mollie" Clemens), died of spotted fever. Her death deeply affected the family, including Sam Clemens, who afterward wrote critically about undertakers and anyone who profited from the death of a loved one. Four days after Jennie's death, he lashed out at the Carson City undertaker who had handled her arrangements, writing a letter to the *Enterprise* that said, in part, "There is a system of extortion going on here which is absolutely terrific . . . does not this undertaker take advantage of that unfortunate delicacy which prevents a man from disputing an unjust bill for services rendered in burying the dead, to extort ten-fold more than his labors are worth?" Three days after Jennie Clemens died, she was buried in Lone Mountain Cemetery in Carson City. A small stone bearing her name, the names of her parents, and the dates of her birth and death still marks her final resting place.

By May 1864, Sam Clemens was growing bored with Virginia City. Nevada archivist Guy Louis Rocha has written that Virginia City had entered an economic slump and Clemens "was restless and anxious to move on." In *Roughing It,* Clemens wrote, "I began to get tired of staying in one place so long."

According to many accounts, Clemens's departure from Virginia City occurred after one of his story hoaxes backfired and the editor of a rival newspaper had challenged him to a duel. Michael Franks, assistant editor of the Mark Twain Project at the Bancroft Library, noted in an essay on the subject, "In an editorial he wrote while drunk one evening, Mark Twain jokingly suggested that the money raised at [a charity ball in

Carson City] was to go not to the Sanitary Commission [a precursor to the Red Cross] but to a 'Miscegenation Society somewhere in the East.'"

He also accused a rival newspaper, the *Virginia City Union,* of not meeting its goals for donations to the Sanitary Fund. After completing the editorial, Clemens was persuaded by his coworkers to pull the item. Unfortunately, a pressman later found the copy and assumed it was supposed to appear, so it was inserted into the paper and published.

Not surprisingly, the charity's women accused of promoting interracial marriage/cohabitation were not amused. Their protests appeared in the *Virginia City Union,* which also angrily denied Clemens's claims about it not fulfilling its charitable obligations. Clemens later wrote that the dispute with the *Union*'s editor, James Laird, became so heated that he challenged Laird to a duel. In his semi-fictional *My Autobiography,* the humorist wrote that the duel was eventually called off, but he fled Virginia City in order to avoid being arrested for violating a new anti-dueling law.

Regardless of the actual reasons, Clemens did depart from Nevada Territory in May 1864 for San Francisco. During the next four years, he returned two more times to Carson City and Nevada. In November 1866, he made an appearance in Carson City during his first major lecture tour, which focused on his journey to the Sandwich Islands (Hawaii) earlier that year. Two years later, he gave a pair of lectures in Carson City (on April 29 and 30, 1868) during another West Coast tour.

Upon his departure from Nevada a few days later, the *Territorial Enterprise* wrote: "Mark Twain leaves this morning for San Francisco. Sorry to see you go, Mark, old boy—but we cannot expect to have you always with us. Go then, where duty calls you, and when the highest pinnacle of fame affords you a resting place remember that in the land of silver and sagebrush there are a host of old friends that rejoice in your success."

Sam Clemens never returned to Nevada. His book about his time in the West, *Roughing It,* was published in 1872. Orion Clemens left Carson City in 1866, after failing to gain the nomination for secretary of state. After a brief stint in Meadow Lake, California, he and Mollie settled in Keokuk, Iowa, where he died in 1897.

Chapter Two

A City Takes Shape

Visibly our new home was a desert, walled in by barren, snow-clad mountains. There was not a tree in sight. There was no vegetation but the endless sagebrush and greasewood. All nature was gray with it.

It was a "wooden" town; its population two thousand souls. The main street consisted of four or five blocks of little white frame stores. . . . They were packed close together, side by side, as if room were scarce in that mighty plain. The sidewalk was of boards that were more or less loose and inclined to rattle when walked upon. In the middle of the town was the "plaza" which is native to all towns beyond the Rocky Mountains—a large, unfenced, level vacancy, with a liberty pole in it, and very useful as a place for public auctions, horse trades, and mass meetings, and likewise for teamsters to camp in.

—MARK TWAIN, Roughing It

Statehood brought prosperity to Carson City. Magazine writer John Penn Curry (no relation to Abraham Curry) wrote in the January 1865 issue of *Gazlay's Pacific Monthly,* "Carson City of 1864 is quite a large and important place. It has a large trade with all parts of the State, has the finest site for a town in the whole territory, and is, at present, the capital. A large quarry of stone having been discovered by Abraham Curry, the place now boasts of splendid stores, court-houses, and dwellings, built of this stone; fine hotels, family mansions, beautiful cottages, and, indeed, a place for Nevada to be proud of."

Even journalist J. Ross Browne, who had written somewhat disparagingly of the community after a visit in 1860, revised his thinking following a return trip in 1864 by noting that "Carson City has enjoyed a very wholesome kind of prosperity since my first visit, if I might be allowed to judge by a casual glance at the new buildings around the Plaza and the many pleasant residences in the suburbs."

By becoming the state capital, Carson City quickly evolved into a community of great hustle and bustle. Nellie Mighels, wife of the editor of the new *Carson Morning Appeal* newspaper, Harry Rust Mighels, later recounted her first impressions of the city upon her arrival in the summer of 1865: "My first sight of Carson made me think of a little toy village, with its tiny one-story houses and its few trees. Looking down, it appeared to me like a doll town and I wondered at the time why the houses were built so small and squat, but I afterward learned that the houses [were] made only one story high on account of strong winds."

She added, "Though Carson was not a very large town, it was surprisingly busy and wide awake, due to the amount of freighting that went on with 14 and 16 mule teams. The driver rode one of the mules and guided the whole team with this one line attached to the lead horse. Every team had a set of bells and the musical jingling made a lovely sound at night."

Curry Goes to Work

Perhaps not surprisingly, Abraham Curry was one of those who took full advantage of all of the opportunities created by the city's status, first as the territorial capital and later as the state capital. In 1861, he had donated use of his Warm Springs Hotel to the state for meetings of the first territorial legislature and provided free transportation to the site, located two miles east of the city. Starting in 1862, he was paid to board prisoners at the Warm Springs Hotel and was appointed warden of the territorial prison. In that role, he was able to utilize prison labor at the sandstone quarry he owned adjacent to the hotel to obtain material and construct many of the city's earliest substantial buildings.

On March 1, 1864, Curry sold the hotel, along with twenty acres, the quarry, tools, horses, and use of a toll road that led from the hotel to town, to the Territory of Nevada to be used as a prison. He was paid $80,000: $20,000 on the purchase date and the remainder in the form of territorial bonds that were later converted into state bonds. The original hotel structure burned down in 1867 and was replaced by the current stone main building of the prison, built using rock quarried on the site. The facility has been expanded and remodeled many times during the past century and a half.

From 1868 to 1873, Nevada's lieutenant governor also served as the

ex-officio warden of the Nevada State Prison in Carson City. Perhaps the most bizarre episode to occur at the prison during its early years happened in 1873, when Lieutenant Governor Frank Denver, who a year earlier had put down a prison break, refused to vacate the prison and turn over the keys to his appointed successor, P. C. Hymen. Denver believed there was ambiguity in the new law that removed the prison warden responsibilities from the lieutenant governor's duties, so he would not relinquish his post.

According to Sam Davis, author of *History of Nevada*, Lieutenant Governor Denver declined to leave the prison despite an order from Governor Lewis Bradley and pleas from the attorney general and the secretary of state, both of whom were on the Board of State Prison Commissioners. In response, Governor Bradley instructed Major General William Van Bokkelen to secure the prison. About sixty soldiers with heavy artillery quickly surrounded the penitentiary. Van Bokkelen asked Denver to surrender and the latter did, saying, according to Davis, "to resist would sacrifice human life and allow the prisoners to escape."

ANOTHER OF ABRAHAM CURRY'S GOALS was to persuade the federal government to construct a U.S. Mint facility in Carson City. He recognized that with the massive amounts of silver and gold being extracted from the Comstock and the high costs of transporting the bullion to the nearest mint in Denver, Colorado, it was only logical that Nevada should have its own mint—and he wanted it located in his town. An additional impetus to build a Nevada-based mint was the loss during the Civil War of several U.S. Mint branch facilities that were located in the Southern states.

In March 1863, Congress passed legislation establishing a mint in the Nevada Territory. Curry pushed hard for the mint to be situated in Carson City, which, he argued, was centrally located near all of the state's most productive mines and could provide all of the services that would be needed. His efforts were successful and the future capital city was selected as the site for the branch mint in late 1863. Unfortunately, the Civil War distracted Washington leaders and the actual construction of the mint was delayed until after the conflict ended two years later.

In 1865, the government purchased land for the mint and appointed a commission to oversee the project. Despite serving as one of the commissioners, Curry submitted a construction bid and was selected as the contractor. Work began in 1866, but proceeded slowly due to funding problems, government red tape, bad weather, and a scarcity of building materials. Originally budgeted at $150,000, the final price tag was $426,787.66 when the three-story stone structure was completed in December 1869. The first coins were struck on the mint's equipment on February 11, 1870.

As the person most familiar with the facility, Curry was hired as the first superintendent of the mint. During construction, he had battled constantly with the government over funding—once even traveling to Washington, D.C., to prompt federal officials to pay their outstanding

The U.S. Mint in Carson City, ca. 1880. (Special Collections, University of Nevada, Reno Libraries)

obligations. Almost immediately after the mint opened, he was forced to counter efforts to close the new operation, including a push by George S. Boutwell, secretary of the U.S. Treasury, who wanted federal mints only in Philadelphia and San Francisco. Fortunately, Nevada's U.S. senators James Nye and William Stewart, along with its sole congressman, Thomas Fitch, were able to preserve the funding.

IN SEPTEMBER 1870, Curry resigned his position in order to be a candidate for the Republican nomination for lieutenant governor. At the time, the lieutenant governor also served as warden of the Nevada State Prison. He was unsuccessful in gaining the nomination and returned to finishing his various construction projects, including many of the commercial buildings in town and a home for his family, which he completed in 1871. Built using sandstone from the prison quarry, Curry's house on the corner of Nevada and Telegraph streets was a simple but elegant rectangular structure that boasted walls that were two feet thick and a large cupola with a skylight.

Curry also remained involved in various other projects, even some that he didn't build. For instance, in 1869, the state legislature approved a bill to establish a Nevada State Orphans Home in Carson City. Shortly after, Curry, along with A. B. Driesbach, George L. Gibson, Aaron D. Treadway, and George Tufly, purchased a seventeen-acre site on what was then the outskirts of town (the corner of Fifth and Stewart streets), which they donated to the state for an orphanage. A two-story wooden Victorian dormitory opened in 1870 and admitted its first child. That structure operated until 1902, when it was destroyed by fire. A second, larger orphanage was built on the site in 1903. It was built using sandstone blocks from the state prison at a cost of $38,000. This impressive three-story building remained open for the next six decades. In 1963, it was demolished and replaced by a complex of small cottages, which served as group foster homes for orphans. The cottages were closed in 1989.

Curry's most ambitious project, however, was construction of the maintenance facilities of the Virginia & Truckee Railroad, which he began in December 1872. Again using sandstone from the prison quarry, Curry erected what he boasted was the largest building in the state of Nevada (163 feet by 60 feet). While commonly referred to as the

The second Nevada State Orphans Home in Carson City, early twentieth century. (Library of Congress)

The V&T Shops (Roundhouse) in Carson City, 1880s. (Special Collections, University of Nevada, Reno Libraries)

V&T Roundhouse, the building was actually rectangular and held nearly a dozen large bays with doors for repairing and maintaining the railroad's locomotives and other equipment. When it was completed in 1873, Curry celebrated by hosting a massive dedication ceremony that included a July 4 Railroad Ball.

The development of the V&T Railroad represented an important milestone in Carson City's history. Efforts to build a railroad to transport Virginia City's ore began in 1861, when the Virginia, Carson & Truckee Railroad Company was chartered to construct a line from Virginia City to the California boundary at Lake Tahoe. This railroad, and several others that were proposed, were never built because of problems in raising the capital. Finally, in May 1867, William Sharon of the Bank of California, which controlled many of Virginia City's mines and mills, incorporated the Virginia & Truckee Rail Road Company to lay a line that would stretch north from Gold Hill, through Virginia City, and along Lousetown Creek to connect with the Central Pacific Railroad at a point on the Truckee River that was ten miles east of the future site of Reno. However, settlers in Carson City and Washoe Valley, which would have been bypassed by the route, strenuously opposed the proposal.

In response, the state legislature authorized Ormsby and Storey counties to issue bonds in the amount of $500,000, which would be given to Sharon if he agreed to re-route the line through Carson City. Sharon agreed and, in March 1868, a new company was created, the Virginia & Truckee Railroad. Work began in February 1869 and was completed between Virginia City and Carson City in January 1870. The line reached the Central Pacific tracks near the banks of the Truckee River in August 1872 and was extended south from Carson City to Minden in 1906.

In addition to locating its maintenance facility in Carson City, V&T officials also placed their main offices in the capital city. A long and narrow yellow train depot–office complex, which today houses several businesses, was constructed on the corner of Carson and East Washington streets. As a result, many V&T executives built fine homes in Carson City, including the railroad's superintendent, Henry M. Yerington, and the railroad's paymaster and general ticket agent, Edward Niles.

For Virginia City, Gold Hill, Silver City, and Carson City residents, the V&T's passenger service was an important link to Reno, where travelers could connect with the Central Pacific railroad line (later, the Southern Pacific) and continue on to more distant destinations. Newspaperman John Taylor Waldorf, who grew up in Virginia City in the 1880s, later wrote about a journey on the train route, which was often called one of the "crookedest" in the world:

> Soon the train was among the hills, the dear old hills with the dull brocade of sagebrush. Hills gave way to mountains. We followed the winding course of the Carson River for miles. Then came the great wide sweep of hills that never fail to delight the eye. The air is clear, and one can see for miles. Hills seem to be piled on hills, mountains

on mountains. The train makes the letter S and the letter U over and over again. Horseshoe bends are too common for distinction. We climb steadily as we creep around the slopes, and soon tunnels on the hillside and heaps of waste rock tell us that we have reached the mining country.

The V&T operated more or less profitably until 1890, when business was so depressed that the railroad could not pay its shareholders a dividend. The company struggled financially during the next several decades as Virginia City's mines were depleted. In 1938, the railroad, which had gradually been selling equipment and rails to pay expenses and reduce costs, went into receivership. Later that year, it discontinued service to Virginia City and, in 1941, the rails on that portion of the route were removed and sold. In January 1949, the railroad applied for permission to abandon its entire operation, which was granted in February 1950. On May 30, 1950, the V&T operated its last train, which ran from Reno to Minden.

Rise of the Silver Dome

Almost concurrent with building the V&T was the construction of the State Capitol between 1870 and 1871. In 1869, the Nevada Legislature agreed the state capital would remain in Carson City (the original constitution had called for a three-year moratorium on building a permanent capitol building) and approved the construction of a state capitol. After selecting architectural plans submitted by San Francisco architect Joseph Gosling, a state commission accepted the low bid submitted by Peter Cavanaugh and Son of Carson City. The state authorized $100,000 for construction and, to keep costs down, agreed to provide sandstone blocks from the state prison quarry at no cost. The cornerstone was laid on June 9, 1870.

Work on the three-story masonry structure, which combined Classical Revival, Renaissance Revival, and Italianate architectural elements, continued for the next eleven months. When completed, the original building was a cruciform with a central rectangle that measured 76 feet wide by 85 feet deep, with two wings measuring 35 feet by 53 feet. The windows were made of French crystal, while the floors and wainscoting were crafted from Alaskan marble. In the original first-floor plan, offices

A postcard image of the Nevada State Capitol with Annex, ca. 1909. (Nevada State Archives)

of the main constitutional officers, such as governor, were located at each corner and connected by central halls. The Nevada Supreme Court and the senate and assembly chambers were located on the second floor. Atop the Capitol was a wooden cupola with a tin-coated, steel-panel octagonal dome. While the dome was initially covered with a fireproof paint called "Princess Red," by 1876 it was painted silver.

Not surprisingly, state government would eventually outgrow the facility and, in 1906, an octagonal-shaped stone addition was built on the east side of the Capitol to house the state library. An ornate two-story breezeway attached the addition to the main structure. Nine years later, the Capitol was again expanded, with longer north and south wings added to the structure. Designed by famed Reno architect Frederic DeLongchamps, the expansion used stone from the same quarry as the original Capitol building. The additions increased the size of the legislative chambers on the second floor as well as the first-floor office space.

By 1937, it had also become obvious that the tiny supreme court chambers on the second floor were inadequate for the court, so a new courthouse was constructed opposite the Capitol on Carson Street. Also designed by DeLongchamps, the 21,000-square-foot Moderne-style building was adequate for the court's needs for many decades. In 1967, the number of justices was increased from three to five, with a corresponding increase in staff, and by the 1980s the court again found that it had outgrown its home. In 1992, the supreme court moved into a modern, 120,000-square-foot building located southeast of the State Capitol.

By the 1960s, the Nevada State Legislature also found the Capitol was no longer adequate for its needs. In 1971, the legislature relocated to new quarters south of the Capitol. The facility, designed by Reno architect Graham Erskine, contained larger chambers for the senate and assembly as well as offices for staff and the legislators. In 1997, the Legislative Building was modernized and expanded to 96,000 square feet.

The Fire Snuffers

With Carson City's development, it quickly became obvious that the city needed basic civic services, such as fire protection. In June 1863, a volunteer fire company was organized that was called Warren Engine Company #1. The name honors a Revolutionary War hero, General Joseph Warren, who fought and died during the Battle of Bunker Hill. Shortly after, two other volunteer fire companies were established, Curry Engine Company #2 (in 1864) and the S.T. Swift Company #3 (in 1873). In *Carson City: Nevada's Capital City,* Willa Oldham said the three companies competed to put out fires (whichever company received credit for being first on the scene received the insurance money for fighting the fire), and "more than one building burned to the ground while rival

The Warren Engine Company No. 1 building, 1940. (Nevada State Archives)

companies engaged in fisticuffs in the street trying to prevent the other company from coupling with the fire cistern."

While the Warren Company was housed in various sites around the community, including the Kitzmeyer Building on Carson Street, the Curry and Swift companies shared a two-story sandstone structure on the corner of Curry and Musser streets that was erected by Abraham Curry in 1863. In 1908, the city authorized the Warren Company to move into the structure previously used by the other two fire companies, which had disbanded by then. It operated in this building until the early 1950s, when the company moved across the street to a new three-bay, two-story structure that became the headquarters station. From the 1950s to the 1990s, the company's historic former home served as a museum displaying photographs and vintage fire equipment and uniforms. In the mid-1990s, the Curry-built structure was renovated and converted into offices for the Nevada secretary of state.

In 1964, the Carson City Fire Department evolved into a blend of full-time professional and volunteer firefighters and hired its first paid fire chief, Les Groth, who had previously been a member of the Warren Company. Over the years, the city has increased the number of professional firefighters on its staff and added new fire stations. In 1994, both the Warren Company and the Carson City Fire Department relocated to a new facility at 777 South Stewart Street (the 1950s-era building was demolished in 2005). Today, the volunteer Warren Company—said to be the oldest continuously operating volunteer fire company in the western U.S.—complements the department's professional staff and assists when needed. The Warren Engine Company #1 Fire Museum is tucked inside the main fire station.

Reading, Writing, and Religion

Once Carson City took root, it quickly became obvious that the community needed to develop schools to educate the young. According to Nevada historian James W. Hulse, a remarkable schoolteacher from Michigan, Hannah K. Clapp, helped establish Carson City's first school in 1861. Called the Sierra Seminary, the innovative private, coeducational school attracted the offspring of many of the community's most prominent families and had a board of directors that included some of the most important figures in the state at the time, including territorial governor (and future U.S. senator) James Nye, attorney (and future U.S. senator) William Stewart, and Territorial Supreme Court justice John W. North. The school operated for about a quarter century.

Clapp was born near Albany, New York, in 1824 and educated at the Union Seminary in Ypsilanti, Michigan. After teaching for several years in Michigan and serving as principal of Lansing's Female Seminary, one of the first female colleges in the state of Michigan, she headed west with her brother and his family. Upon arriving in Carson City in 1860—she had earlier accepted a teaching job in Vacaville, California—she saw the critical need for schools in the newly minted Nevada Territory. She canceled her Vacaville plans and soon organized the Sierra Seminary, which was chartered by the territorial legislature in November 1861.

Hannah Clapp, ca. 1876. (Nevada Historical Society)

Clapp became part of Carson City folklore in 1875, when she and her partner, Eliza C. Babcock, were the low bidders for the contract to construct an iron fence around the State Capitol. According to a popular legend, she submitted the bid using her initials so as not to be disqualified for being a woman. But, former Nevada state archivist Guy Louis Rocha points out, "the population of the entire county was listed as only 3,222 souls in the 1875 state census. The truth is almost everybody knew H. K. Clapp . . . virtually every city directory and newspaper story referred to Hannah as H. K. Clapp."

In 1877, Clapp and Babcock, who co-operated the Sierra Seminary, returned from a trip to the East Coast excited about the then-new concept of "kindergartens" and opened the state's first such program. A decade later, at an age when most people would be at least contemplating the winding down of a long and successful career, the sixty-three-year-old Clapp became the first staff member hired at the relocated University of Nevada (which had moved from Elko to Reno). In addition to teaching history and English, her duties included managing the women's dormitory and operating the school library.

During her life, Clapp was also a devoted suffragist. She worked tirelessly to pass a Nevada voting rights act for women during every legislative session between 1883 and 1899. Unfortunately, it wouldn't be until 1914 that the state finally approved legislation allowing women to vote in state elections (the Nineteenth Amendment granting women the right to vote in federal elections was not ratified until 1920).

In 1901, Clapp retired to Palo Alto, California. When she died in 1908, the *Reno Evening Gazette* editorialized that "it is doubtful if any single individual has had a wider influence in the forming days of Nevada than Miss Clapp."

IN ADDITION to the Sierra Seminary, Carson City established a pair of public schools. In his 1883 memoir, pioneer Carson City resident Jacob Klein noted, "There was a small public school here. . . . It was held in a little stone house [often referred to as the Stone Schoolhouse] situated south-east of my brewery." Additionally, Willa Oldham reported that "when Nevada became a state in 1864, Ormsby County's potential school population was reported to be 512 children between the ages of 4 and 21; 125 attended private schools and 173 attended the two public schools." In about 1872, a two-story wooden schoolhouse called the Central School was built on the corner of Minnesota and Telegraph streets. At the time it was the largest school in town, housing grades one through twelve. According to Carson City historical writer Scott Schrantz, there were a couple of smaller schools on the edges of town, the North Ward and South Ward schools, but the Central School quickly became the community's primary education facility. In 1906, the original Central School was replaced by a larger brick structure, which was located on the corner of Musser and Division streets. The second Central School, which covered an entire city block, remained standing until the 1970s, although it ceased being used as a high school in 1937.

OF COURSE, as the city evolved it addressed its other needs, including those of a more spiritual nature. Carson City's first organized religious body was a Methodist congregation, which began meeting at the Eagle Valley Ranch in 1859. Other organized religious congregations soon followed, including Roman Catholic (1860), Presbyterian (1861), and Episcopal (1863).

Jacob Klein, who arrived in the community in 1860, said the first church building erected in Carson City was a wooden Roman Catholic church on King Street. Strong winds knocked down that structure two years later and it was replaced by a sturdier wooden building in 1871. In the 1970s, the church was enlarged and rebuilt with a brick façade. In 2001, following the construction of a new church, the older building was deconsecrated and sold to the nonprofit Brewery Arts Center.

The Presbyterian congregation originally met in the Stone School-house. Despite several prominent Carson City residents as members, including Orion Clemens and William M. Stewart, funds to build a church were slow in coming. Construction began in 1862 but was still not completed by 1864, due to a lack of money. That year, church trustees asked Samuel Clemens (Mark Twain) if he would present his Third Annual Message to the Third House (a mock legislative meeting held by media members and lobbyists following the regular legislative sessions) as a church fundraiser. Clemens agreed, noting in a letter to the trustees: "Certainly. If the public can find anything in a grave state paper worth paying a dollar for, I am willing they should pay that amount or any other."

Since the church was not yet completed, Clemens delivered his address on the second floor of the Ormsby County Courthouse. It was

The First Presbyterian Church of Carson City, 1940s. (Special Collections, University of Nevada, Reno Libraries)

reported that he raised about $200 with the speech, which helped provide the funds needed to finish the structure later that year. The original brick structure on North Nevada Street was remodeled and expanded in 1896. By 2006, the historic church had grown too small for the congregation and was badly in need of repairs, so there was talk of demolishing the building. Public outcry persuaded the congregation to drop those plans and build a new, larger sanctuary behind the original church. City officials also provided funds in 2006 and 2009 to restore and preserve the original structure.

In 1867, Carson City's Methodists completed their church, an imposing stone monolith with a tall wooden spire erected on the corner of Division and Musser streets. The structure was built using sandstone blocks from Abraham Curry's quarry. Over the years, the church has remained largely unchanged except for the removal of the wooden spire and an addition on the west side.

St. Peter's Episcopal Church was the last of Carson City's quartet of historic houses of worship to be built. Constructed in 1867–68, the wooden Gothic Revival structure on North Division Street, which is notable for its enormous steeple and New England–influenced design, is the state's oldest Episcopal church. A historic structure report released in 2008 noted that the building had been expanded in 1873–74 as well as in 1890–91 and 1911.

Carson's Commercial Core

Carson City's commercial district also began to take shape, largely to the north of the capital plaza site. In addition to the Ormsby House hotel and Curry's Great Basin Hotel, the city's budding downtown saw the construction of several substantial brick structures including the Cheek & Holland Furniture Store, believed to be the oldest commercial building still standing in Carson City (1861), the two-story Muller Hotel and the three-story St. Charles Hotel (1862), the White House Hotel (1862), the Corbett House (1865), the Carson Brewing Company (1865), the Olcovich Brothers Dry Goods Store (about 1870), and the Kitzmeyer Furniture Factory (1873).

The side-by-side Muller and St. Charles hotels, both still in use, were constructed, respectively, by Albert Muller, and George Remington

Carson Street, 1870s.
(Special Collections,
University of Nevada,
Reno Libraries)

and Dan Plitt. The larger St. Charles became the main stagecoach stop in Carson City and, when it opened, was considered one of the most elegant hotels in the state. It advertised itself as the "pleasantest resort in Carson and where everything kept by the bar is the best quality." On the first floor, the hotel boasted a small restaurant and saloon, while the upper floors contained about forty rooms (numbers vary). The Muller was a more "working class" joint that apparently catered primarily to French Canadian woodcutters.

Over the years, the two hotels had many changes in name and ownership. In 1866, a fire damaged both structures, but they were soon repaired and reopened. In the 1870s, the St. Charles was owned and operated by George Tufly and his wife, who gained a reputation for offering quality accommodations and meals. An interesting historical side note is that during the time the Tuflys owned the hotel, they would often allow a local countertenor, Richard Jose, to sing Cornish ballads in exchange for meals. Jose eventually married their granddaughter and later became a famous performer in New York and a pioneering recording artist.

The Muller and St. Charles (renamed the Briggs Hotel in 1891) were consolidated in 1894 and became known as the Briggs House. During the next century, the hotel gradually declined. By 1910, the business, using the name Golden West Hotel, was often described as a flop house that served poor-quality meals and had run-down accommodations. In the mid-twentieth century, the name changed to the Travelers Hotel, then to the Pony Express Hotel. Finally, in the 1990s, businessman Robert McFadden purchased the decrepit hotel. He renovated the structure, upgraded the ground-floor restaurant, and reclaimed the original St. Charles name. In 2004, Jenny and Mark Lopiccolo bought the historic place, which they remodeled and restored. Today, the upper rooms are once again available for nightly lodging while the downstairs hosts the Firkin and Fox pub.

Unfortunately, not all of Carson City's historic hostelries from that era have been as fortunate as the St. Charles and Muller. The White House Hotel on the northeast corner of Third and Plaza streets managed to survive nearly to 1964 before it was demolished after a fire. Today, the former site of the hotel is near the Supreme Court Building at the Capitol Complex. Likewise, the Corbett House is gone, destroyed by fire in 1876.

Another important commercial structure from Carson's early years that still exists is the Olcovich Brothers Dry Good Store at Fourth and South Carson streets. The one-story brick structure incorporates two storefronts and has often been divided into two separate businesses. Hyman, Joseph, Herman, and Benjamin Olcovich offered a wide variety of products in their store, including carpets, furniture, groceries, and shoes as well as imported teas, coffees, cigars, and spices.

The Olcovich brothers were part of a small but successful colony of Jewish merchants and businessmen who settled in Carson City in the late 1850s and early 1860s. Many had close affiliations with suppliers in California. In his book, *Jews in Nevada: A History,* historian John P. Marschall said that a Hebrew Benevolent Society was formed in Carson City in 1862 to help newly arriving Jews find work and accommodations. By the late 1870s, Carson City's Jewish population had stabilized at about ninety. Other prominent Jewish businessmen in the capital city during this period included Abraham Klauber and Francis Mandelbaum, who owned a successful clothing and general store; Joseph Platt, who also owned a clothing shop and whose son, Samuel, would become a U.S. attorney and perennial political candidate; Joseph Rosenstock (men's and boy's clothing store); and Jacob Klein (brewery).

By the end of the nineteenth century, when Nevada was deep into an economic slump caused by the decline of the state's mining industry, nearly all of Carson City's Jewish merchants had moved on to more promising communities in California and other states. The Olcovich brothers closed their business in the early part of the century and sold the corner portion to William Reker to be used as a saloon. They leased the rest of the space out for a candy factory. In the 1920s, the Carson Theater replaced the candy business. In 1931, John Gulling bought the saloon and remodeled the building for his Capital Mortuary, which it remained for many years. By the 1990s, the mortuary was gone, replaced by an antiques store. Today, the whole building is the home of a popular coffeehouse.

Nearly as old is the former Kitzmeyer Furniture Factory building on the corner of Carson and Plaza streets. This two-story brick structure housed a furniture manufacturing company owned by George W. Kitzmeyer from 1873 to 1900. Following his death, his son, George E. Kitzmeyer, continued the furniture business, which had long included coffins, but added undertaking services. Within a few years, the latter had become more profitable than the former and the younger Kitzmeyer converted the business into a mortuary. The building was remodeled in the 1930s to meet the needs of the expanding business. By the 1980s, the mortuary was long gone and the former furniture factory was being used as a delicatessen. It has continued to house restaurant businesses in recent years.

One of the city's most historic commercial structures is the Carson Brewing Company building, erected by the owners of the state's first brewery. The large, two-story brick edifice, which sits on the southwest corner of King and Division streets, originally housed the brewery operations on the first floor and a bar and lodge room on the upper floor. The brewery was started in 1860 by John Wagner, and he was later joined by Jacob Klein; the company provided barrels, kegs, and bottles of beer to Carson City and Virginia City saloons. By 1877, Klein had bought out his partners and become sole owner of the brewery, which specialized in steam beer, a type of beer not requiring refrigeration when made. Following Klein's death in 1899, the brewery was sold to James Raycraft and Frank Golden, who operated it for about a decade before selling it to Max Stenz, who previously owned the Goldfield Brewery.

Stenz converted from steam beer to lager and changed the name of his product to "Tahoe Beer," with the slogan "Famous as the Lake." Stenz also began bottling soft drinks and mineral water from Carson Hot Springs, and started packaging and selling artificial ice. During Prohibition, the

brewery created a popular "near-beer," a low-alcohol beverage that could be legally sold. Arnold A. Millard, Stenz's son-in-law, began managing the brewery in 1926. To keep the company afloat, Millard went into the coal, wood, fuel oil, and ice businesses.

The end of Prohibition in 1933 gave a temporary boost to the brewery, which replaced much of its old equipment. However, during the 1940s, the beer business underwent a major consolidation, with large national brands pushing aside the small local operators. In 1948, Millard closed the brewery for good.

The brewery building was sold to the Donrey Media Group, owner of the local *Nevada Appeal* newspaper. From 1951 to 1975, the *Appeal* was produced and printed in the building. In 1976, Carson City acquired the building and leased it to the nonprofit Brewery Arts Center.

The former suds-making factory was gradually converted into a performing arts venue and art center that today hosts more than one hundred events annually. The center also houses the operations of Access Carson City Charter Cable channels 10 and 26 as well as the Artisans Café & Gift Shop. The center's programs include BAC Stage Kids, the Brewery Arts Center Summer Stock Theater, the Jazz and Beyond music festival, Concerts at the Brewery, Classes at the Brewery, and the Artisans store. Several independent community arts groups also use the center, including Proscenium Players, Inc., and the King Street Fine Arts Gallery. With the help of private donors and a city grant, the center purchased the former St. Teresa of Avila Catholic Church in 2001 and converted it into a performance hall. In 2008, the center announced plans to link the two facilities, separated by South Minnesota Street, with a $3.5 million expansion that would include a 400-seat amphitheater. Under the plan, the city would abandon a 170-foot stretch of the street so the center could expand between its two properties.

Carson City's Newspapers

Mark Twain wasn't the only significant figure in early Nevada journalism with a connection to Carson City. In fact, two, Harry Mighels and Sam Davis, are still considered giants in the state's newspaper industry. Additionally, as University of Nevada, Reno, journalism professor Jake Highton has written, there were other, less-remembered editors who were equally influential in their time, including Richard R. "Deacon" Parkinson and William J. Forbes.

While Nevada's first newspaper was a handwritten sheet called the *Gold-Cañon Switch* that was produced in Johntown (near present-day Silver City) in 1854, the first true printed newspaper was the *Territorial Enterprise,* published in Genoa on December 18, 1858. The *Enterprise* was relocated to Carson City in November 1859, where it became the first newspaper to be published in the future capital. According to historians Richard E. Lingenfelter and Karen Rix Gash, the paper's owners were not good businessmen and, in July 1860, creditors assumed control and sold the business to Henry DeGroot. He, in turn, sold it to Jonathan Williams, one of the earlier owners, who moved the paper to Virginia City in October 1860.

But Carson City was not without a newspaper for long. In December 1860, John C. Lewis began publishing the weekly *Silver Age.* About nine months later, the paper's frequency was increased and it became Nevada's first daily newspaper. The *Silver Age* was apparently well received in the community but did not prove particularly long-lived. Publication ceased in November 1862 and the press and other equipment were moved to Virginia City to establish another newspaper, the *Virginia Daily Union.*

About nine months after the departure of *Silver Age,* another newspaper publisher took a crack at producing a publication in the capital city. W. W. Ross established the *Carson Daily Independent* in July 1863. The paper struggled through various format, frequency, and ownership changes before failing in October 1864. It was followed by the *Daily Morning Post,* which lasted only from August 1864 to about May 1865.

Carson City's newspaper situation finally settled down for a short time with the publication of the *Carson Daily Appeal* in May 1865. Owned by E. F. McElwain, J. Barrett, and Marshall Robinson and edited by Harry Mighels, who had previously edited the *Marysville Appeal,* the paper quickly established its Republican political views by announcing the capture of Jefferson Davis, president of the Confederacy.

In December 1870, the *Carson Daily Appeal* was sold to C. L. Perkins and H. C. Street, who changed its name to the *Daily State Register* and its politics to Democrat. Meanwhile Mighels and Robinson, with the backing of U.S. Senate candidate John P. Jones (who won), started the *New Daily Appeal* in September 1872. Three months later, they bought and ceased publishing the rival *Daily State Register.* In 1873, the word "New" was dropped and five years later Mighels became the sole owner.

Under Mighels, the *Daily Appeal* became one of the state's most influential papers. Mighels editorialized against the excess of the railroads and, according to Myron Angel in Thompson & West's *History of Nevada,* "penned the purest and best of English, and leveled all opposition by his masterly logic. His wit and repartee flashed like the diamond. His invective was an avalanche." Comstock editor C. C. Goodwin later wrote that Mighels, who died in 1879 of stomach cancer, "was a decided genius, and he was growing mentally every day." Another Comstock editor, Wells Drury, noted that Mighels's editorials "were winged words and he had a profound grasp of political affairs. His philosophical ruminations were original, spontaneous, brand new and with the unmistakable stamp of genius upon them and minted from the brain of a scholar and a gentleman."

Following his death, ownership of the *Daily Appeal* shifted to his widow, Nellie Verrill Mighels, who had helped her husband publish the paper for many years. Harry Mighels had taught his wife how to set newspaper type and, to save money, how to take notes and report the news. "We couldn't afford to pay a reporter $25 a month, so I did it myself," she later recalled. "It wasn't so hard—my husband had taught me to write down high spots of a speech. By the time the speaker had quit orating and had come to another high spot, I would be through writing the first high spot. By that method, I managed to give an accurate account of the proceedings."

In 1877 and 1879, Nellie Mighels covered the Nevada Legislature—she was the first woman to do so. After her husband's death, Nellie hired Samuel Post Davis as editor of the newspaper (she married him in 1880). Like Harry Mighels, Davis fought the railroads and was an energetic advocate of a free press, often battling the closed-door meetings of government bodies. Highton notes that in 1892, Davis went to jail for a brief period for refusing to reveal his sources for a story he wrote about county officials receiving bribes from companies awarded government contracts.

Sam P. Davis, 1889. (Special Collections, University of Nevada, Reno Libraries)

An interesting side note concerns Davis's younger brother, Robert, who worked as a printer's devil (apprentice) at the *Appeal* when he was a young man. Robert later worked as a reporter in San Francisco, then moved to New York, where he became a feature writer for the *New York World* and the *New York Journal*. In 1903, he was hired as an editor of *Munsey's Magazine* and, later, of Munsey's *All-Story Weekly*. In that role, he nurtured and published a number of popular fiction writers, including Edgar Rice Burroughs (*Tarzan*), Alfred Merritt, Max Brand, and Ray Cummings. From the 1920s until his death in 1942 at the age of seventy-three, the younger Davis wrote a popular newspaper column for the *New York Sun* titled "Bob Davis Recalls."

Sam Davis quit newspapering in 1898, after he was elected Nevada state controller. According to Highton, "he was not only an honest politician, he was a good, tough one." During his two terms in office, he fought insurance companies that tried to renege on their obligations to their customers following the 1906 San Francisco earthquake and made one New York insurance company repay its shareholders $250,000 that had been—at least in his mind—improperly donated to President William McKinley's campaign fund.

After Davis's departure, the *Daily Appeal* was leased to Harry Mighels Jr., son of the former owner (and Davis's stepson), who operated it until 1906. During the next several years the paper was leased by a number of different individuals but remained under the ownership of the Mighels-

Davis family until 1938. Since then, the paper, which is now known as the *Nevada Appeal,* has been owned by several individuals and entities, including the Swift Newspaper chain, which acquired it in 1995. The *Appeal* is considered Carson City's oldest business and the longest continually published newspaper in the state.

Three other noteworthy newspapers in Carson City's journalism story include the *Daily Nevada Tribune,* started in July 1872; the *Carson City News,* which began publishing in June 1891; and the *Carson City Sun,* founded in 1880 by youngsters Selig and Isaac Olcovich. The *Tribune* was owned by Richard R. "Deacon" Parkinson, his son, Edward, and James McClure. For a time, the paper carried on an enthusiastic rivalry with the *Appeal* that resulted in an 1874 duel with pistols between the *Appeal's* editor, David Sessions, and Edward Parkinson. Fortunately, neither died but Sessions suffered a shattered hand while the younger Parkinson was wounded in the leg.

The war of words between the two papers continued for the next two decades, until the Parkinsons leased the paper to Hal A. Lemmon in November 1894 and relocated to Seattle. The paper sputtered along for another two years before it was sold to C. A. Norcross, who moved it to Reno, where it faded away.

Carson City lawyer Edwin T. Dupuis founded the *Carson City News* as a weekly paper. Less than a year after he started it, Dupuis sold the publication to Annie Hudnall Martin, who also served as its editor. In November 1895, Martin sold the paper to H. C. Dunn and Hal Lemmon (former lessees of the *Tribune*), who operated it for nearly a decade. In 1905, the paper was sold to the first of about half a dozen owners or lessees who would operate it more or less successfully for the next quarter century. Finally, in 1930 it was sold to Harry Mighels Jr., owner of the *Appeal,* who merged it with his paper.

The *Carson City Sun* was a semiweekly created by ten-year-old Selig Olcovich and twelve-year-old Isaac Olcovich (sons of Hyman and Pauline Olcovich). The two served as editors for the paper, which, according to Marschall, "never missed an opportunity to note when a Jewish person visited or left the area." In 1891, the paper expanded in size and frequency, and changed its name to the *Carson City Weekly.* In 1898, Isaac left the paper to work in his family's business. When Selig tried to raise the annual subscription rate for the paper to $1.50 per year, he lost nearly all of his customers. The *Weekly* folded in January 1899.

Abe's Legacy

On October 19, 1873, Abraham Curry died of a stroke at the age of fifty-eight. Alf Doten wrote in the *Gold Hill News:* "Carson City will miss 'Uncle Abe.' To him more than to any man is that beautiful village indebted for its existence and success." Despite being involved not only in the founding of Carson City but also in the construction of many of its significant buildings, Curry died nearly broke. His penchant for sharing the wealth—he hosted numerous ceremonial balls and special events—as well as poor business decisions prevented him from getting rich or leaving much to his family.

Doris Cerveri reports that Curry's send-off was "one of the grandest pageants in the State of Nevada." The founder of Carson City was buried in the Lone Mountain Cemetery but because his family had no money to buy a tombstone, there was little to indicate the site of his grave until 1964, when a large stone with a plaque was donated by the Nevada Highway Department.

Curry's entire estate at the time of his death consisted of his house on Nevada Street and nine vacant lots in one of the subdivisions he developed. To fend off creditors, Mary Curry filed a homestead notice to prevent them from taking the house. Cerveri says that two of Curry's daughters supported Mary during the next four decades but "times were always hard for the women Curry left behind, as their lack of money remained a serious problem." Mary Curry suffered a stroke in 1911, which left her paralyzed, and she died July 29, 1912, at the age of ninety-four.

Ormsby County's Forgotten Towns: Lakeview and Empire

Many people don't realize that the former Ormsby County (now part of the consolidated city-county of Carson City) once was home to other communities in addition to Carson City. For example, the Virginia and Gold Hill Water Company established the tiny hamlet of Lakeview in 1870. Located in the hills at the northern end of Eagle Valley, where it meets Washoe Valley, Lakeview was a link in an elaborate and ingenious flume, tunnel, and pipe system that transported water from Marlette

Lake and the Hobart Reservoir above Lake Tahoe to Virginia City. Its name reflected the fact that it overlooked Washoe Lake. In 1873, the Virginia & Truckee Railroad built the Lakeview Station as part of its route from Reno to Carson City. A post office opened in Lake View, as it was then called, in 1881 but closed two years later. A second post office, this time called Lakeview, opened in 1890 but it also was short-lived, closing in 1894. Lakeview never grew to more than a handful of homes and buildings. Today, the name is associated with a residential neighborhood on the west side of U.S. 395.

A more substantial Ormsby County community was Empire City, located on the north bank of the Carson River, about four miles east of Carson City. In the mid-1850s, Nicholas "Dutch Nick" Ambrosia opened a small tavern and trading post on the site to cater to travelers on the Overland Trail. In 1860, he and a partner, William H. Mead, surveyed a town site that they named Empire City. The community quickly grew, thriving because of its proximity to the half dozen lumber and ore mills that were built along the Carson River, including the Mexican Mill, the Morgan Mill, and the Silver State Mill. At one point, there was so much logging business that the settlement was nicknamed "Seaport." According to some reports, Empire City had about seven hundred residents during the decade of 1865 to 1875, as well as hotels, an elementary school, saloons, stables, dry goods stores, and other businesses. The

Families survey the damage during the Empire Flood of 1907. (Special Collections, University of Nevada, Reno Libraries)

Virginia & Truckee Railroad also established an Empire City station on its route between Carson City and Virginia City. A post office opened in 1866, although the name was shortened to Empire in 1895.

While the decline of mining in Virginia City was the primary reason for Empire City's ultimate demise, another factor was its location near the Carson River, which regularly flooded the community. One of the worst floods occurred in March 1907, when a series of storms hit northern Nevada. The storms started out as snow but warmed into rain, which soon caused severe flooding. According to a United States Geological Survey report, "rain fell across the entire watershed, even the highest mountain crests. Extensive damage occurred." The USGS said that residents living near the river or in low areas were forced to move to higher ground. The Carson River crested with a discharge of about four thousand cubic feet per second at Empire, destroying several bridges and a dam that had been used by mills for mining and ore processing. Photographs show homes half submerged in the floodwaters and young boys on rafts floating down the streets.

The Empire City post office finally closed in 1912 and the site of the town quickly melted into the sagebrush. Today, a newer neighborhood, called New Empire, is situated near the former town location. Additionally, the historic Empire Cemetery still remains on a hillside overlooking the Carson River (off Sheep Drive). The old cemetery has dozens of well-maintained graves, many with substantial marble headstones and wrought iron fences. An estimated two hundred people, most of whom died in the late nineteenth century, are buried in the cemetery.

One of Empire City's most famous residents was Edwin Ewing Roberts (generally known as E. E. Roberts), who later became Nevada's U.S. congressman (the state had only one congressional representative prior to the 1980s). Late in his life, Roberts also served as a popular Reno mayor. E. E. Roberts came to Nevada in 1897 to witness the heavyweight boxing match in Carson City between Jim Corbett and Bob Fitzsimmons. He liked what he saw, particularly the libertarian views of most of the state's residents, and took a teaching position in Empire City. Two years later, Roberts passed the Nevada State Bar and was elected district attorney of Ormsby County. In 1910, Roberts was elected Nevada's representative to Congress, an office he held until 1918. After practicing law for a number of years—he specialized in divorce cases—Roberts returned to politics in 1923 with his election as Reno's mayor. During his term he scandalized the nation, and amused many Reno citizens, by calling for an end to Prohibition and enthusiastically endorsing the state's legalization of gambling in 1931. He died in office in 1933 and is buried in Reno.

Chapter Three

Culture and Community in Eagle Valley

Carson City, smallest of State capitals, was biggest in importance (in the view of elated Carsonites, anyway).

—WELLS DRURY, *An Editor on the Comstock Lode*

$\mathcal{B}$y the mid-1870s, Carson City was truly becoming a proper community and cementing its status as the seat of state government. The city was formally incorporated in 1875 and elected its first city officials. The state capital had already seen a couple of legislative sessions and Nevada's second governor, Lewis R. Bradley, was nearing the end of his first term (he would serve two). It was a time when the community began to fill in; homes of the city's most prominent citizens were built, many on the west side of town, and some of the city's signature public buildings were constructed.

Perhaps the most impressive personal residence ever erected in Carson City was lumberman Duane L. Bliss's home on West Robinson Street, completed in 1879. At the time it was built, the massive three-story Victorian house was the grandest private home in the state. Construction materials were assembled over a six-year period, although it took only months to actually build the structure. It has been reported that three train cars full of bricks were used to build the home's four impressive chimneys, and marble was brought from Italy, Vermont, and Georgia for the seven fireplaces. The wood used to construct the house was furniture-grade white sugar pine that came from Bliss's mills. Additionally, the Bliss Mansion featured all the latest gadgets, such as gas lighting and heating—it was the first residence in Carson City with both—as well as a

telephone relay system linking the house to Bliss's downtown office and his operations at Glenbrook.

While not quite as elaborate, other fine residences were also built during this time, including the Mathias Rinckel Mansion, the Governor Reinhold Sadler House, the Alfred Chartz House, and the Beck-Barber-Belnap House. The last, an elegant two-story house built in the Second Empire architectural style with a mansard roof, was erected in 1875 by lawyer Henry Hudson Beck, who apparently lived there for only a short time. Within a year of building it, Beck sold it to Gold Hill merchant Oscar Barber. In the late 1870s, Supreme Court justice Charles Henry Belnap purchased the house.

Meanwhile, downtown Carson City was also continuing to evolve. In 1877, Daniel and William Corbett built the Arlington Hotel on Carson Street to replace a smaller lodging house that had burned down a year earlier. The Arlington, a two-story brick structure that covered nearly a city block (between Spear and Robinson streets), earned a reputation as one of the city's finest places to stay. On its ground floor, it boasted retail space and a restaurant. The hotel existed until 1966, when the owners decided it was cheaper to tear the aging property down than to renovate it. Today, the site is covered by the Carson Nugget's west parking lot.

From 1893 to about 1900, the Arlington Hotel was home to the Carson

For many decades, Carson City's Arlington Hotel, seen here in the 1940s, was one of the state's premier lodging houses. (Special Collections, University of Nevada, Reno Libraries)

City branch of the Keeley Institute, a franchise medical treatment center that claimed to cure alcoholism and other addictions. Founded in 1879 by Dr. Leslie Keeley, a former Civil War surgeon, the private institute offered a two- to four-week program during which participants were injected four times a day with a proprietary serum, called the "Double Chloride of Gold Remedy," which allegedly would permanently cure the craving for alcohol, nicotine, or opiates. The exact contents of the chloride of gold elixir were secret but it was known to contain diluted amounts of arsenic and strychnine. At its peak in the mid-1890s, the Keeley Institute, which was headquartered in Dwight, Illinois, had thirty-three treatment centers across the U.S. and made Dr. Keeley a millionaire. It is considered the first successful franchised addiction treatment facility—and, in the eyes of many, the first profitable business based on medical quackery.

For a time, the Carson City branch of the institute did a booming business, and its three dozen local owners included many prominent citizens, among them Dr. S. L. Lee, Henry M. Yerington, superintendent of the Virginia & Truckee Railroad, Sam Davis, owner of the *Carson Appeal,* and Dr. J. W. Fox. Following Dr. Keeley's death in 1900, however, the centers began to close, including the one in Carson—largely due to the fact that the treatment was not particularly effective.

Not all of Carson City's development in the 1870s was downtown or on the west side. In 1875–76, jeweler and amateur weatherman Charles Friend erected the state's first weather observatory adjacent to his home on what is now the eastern corner of Stewart and E. King streets. The observatory, which is no longer there, consisted of a small domed tower-like structure that was equipped with a six-inch refracting telescope (borrowed from the U.S. Naval Academy) and weather instruments. After 1887, Friend served as the state's official weather service director—the only one ever—and worked with the U.S. Army Signal Corps to set up more than three dozen weather stations throughout the state.

Buildings of a more institutional nature that were erected in the last quarter of the nineteenth century included the Old State Printing Building, built between 1885 and 1886, the federal post office and government building (1891), and the Stewart Indian School (1890). The Old State Printing Building, now sharing a wall with the Nevada State Library and Archives Building (directly east of the State Capitol), housed the State Printing Office for several decades and, later, the Nevada State Archives and *Nevada Magazine*. Today, it hosts an art gallery with rotating exhibits and the Nevada State Historic Preservation Office. The two-story rectangular structure with tall arched windows was built using sandstone from the prison quarry, so it closely matches the design and appearance of both the State Capitol and the former U.S. Mint.

The old Federal Courthouse and Post Office, early twentieth century, now the Paul Laxalt State Building. (Nevada Commission on Tourism)

The federal post office and government building was designed by Mifflin E. Bell, a prominent nineteenth-century government architect who developed similar post offices in Pittsburgh and Brooklyn. The three-story red-brick and sandstone Victorian-style structure, which cost $134,605, has a unique three-faced clock in a tower on the northwest corner. The last court case was heard in the building in 1965, after which the federal court moved to Reno. The post office moved to new quarters in Carson City in 1970. A few years later, the Nevada State Library moved into the building and remained there until the early 1990s. The structure was completely restored in the mid-1990s and became home of the Nevada Commission on Tourism and *Nevada Magazine*. In 2000, it was renamed the Paul Laxalt State Building in honor of former U.S. senator and Nevada governor Paul Laxalt, who grew up in Carson City.

Carson Culture

Carson City's cultural scene first emerged with the construction of the first Carson Opera House at Carson and Spear streets in 1878. It hosted not only opera performances but also lectures and Shakespearean plays. The opera house lasted about a decade at that site before it was either torn down or relocated when U.S. postal officials bought the opera house's original location for a post office and federal courthouse building, which was completed in 1891.

As for the second Carson Opera House, built in 1888 at Telegraph and Plaza streets, this two-story wooden structure had a spacious dancing hall, four dressing rooms, gaslights, and a theater with seating for up to eight hundred people. It offered musical performances from 1888 until the 1920s, when it was converted into a movie theater. It was destroyed in a fire caused by a faulty furnace in April 1931.

One of the most noteworthy Carson City residents to be associated with the opera house was John P. Meder, who served as manager of the facility for many years and directed many local theater productions. J. P. Meder, as he was also called, arrived in Carson City in the mid-1860s and a few years later was hired as freight agent of the Virginia & Truckee Railroad. Active in local politics—he served on the school board for sixteen years—he was also a talented musician who performed in a local band and composed dozens of waltzes and "schottisches" (Victorian-era

folk dance music). His best-known works included the "Hank Monk Schottische," "My Own Waltz," and "Pretty Blue Eyes Schottische." His father, Benjamin H. Meder, was a prominent local businessman and political figure.

In addition to opera and musical performances, Carson City residents also had other forms of recreation. For instance, the ten-acre farm owned by Aaron Draper Treadway on the west side of the community (roughly bordered by today's Washington, Mountain, Fleischmann, and Minnesota streets) was an extremely popular place for picnics and day outings. Treadway, who had originally traveled west to prospect for gold in California, bought the land in 1861 and planted fast-growing cottonwood trees, some of which can still be found on the site, as well as a fine orchard with peach, pear, apple, and plum trees. He built a small stockyard for horses, cows, oxen, and hogs, as well as a small reservoir that he filled with catfish. Over time, he acquired additional property, including about 300 acres of forest located three miles west of Carson City and 110 acres of land directly west of the community.

In 1866, "Farmer" Treadway opened his ten-acre ranch to the public, offering, for a nominal fee, use of his shaded lands for picnics and games.

When the Virginia & Truckee Railroad was built through Carson City, it skirted the southern border of his property; this proximity allowed groups to run train excursions to his ranch, which became known as Treadway Park (it was during a time when Carson City had no public parks). For example, in 1881, the *Carson Appeal* reported that the Reno Athletic Club would be gathering at the park for its annual athletic competition. The story said that there would be "handsome" prizes for the contestants as well as much "jollification."

In the summer of 1898, the park was converted into Camp Clark, a compound for Nevada volunteers training to fight in the Spanish-American War. The conflict, however, lasted only from April to August of 1898, so the war ended before any Nevada troops could be sent to the battlefield. By late October of that year, all of the trainees had been discharged from duty.

On January 30, 1903, Treadway died. After his death, the farm was sold and the land was developed. In 1949, a large portion of the former ranch/park became the home of the first Carson-Tahoe Hospital, built for $80,000. A single doctor, three nurses, an X-ray technician, a laboratory technologist, a cook, and a janitor staffed the new facility. In November 1968, construction was completed on a new, much larger hospital on the site. At the time, the hospital set aside a small parcel of land on the corner of William and Minnesota streets, which it called Treadway Park, in honor of the original owner. The little park, which is less than an acre, contained some of the original cottonwoods planted by Treadway more than a century ago.

An Amazing Discovery at the State Prison

Few stories involving Carson City are as bizarre as the events surrounding the discovery of so-called prehistoric human footprints in about 1880. Inmates chipping away at the sandstone quarry on the grounds of the Nevada State Prison began turning up footprints pressed into the ancient stone. While most were small and clearly made by animals, one set of prints defied easy explanation. The prints were much larger, reportedly eighteen to twenty inches long, and resembled human footprints. At the urging of prison officials, the California Academy of Sciences in San Francisco was asked to study the prints and determine what might have

made them. In 1882, Charles Drayton Gibbes, the academy's curator of mineralogy, and Dr. Harvey W. Harkness, a mycologist and natural historian, visited the quarry and made cloth impressions of the footprints.

According to a *New York Times* article of August 18, 1882, which carried the headline "Footprints of Monster Men," the two scientists "found six series of tracks of man in regular order, and each showing more or less plainly, the imprint of a sandal . . . in its outline the impression follows clearly the shape of the human foot." In a paper he presented to the academy, Dr. Harkness said the prints dated to the Pliocene period (5.4 to 2.4 million years ago) and noted that the sandal appeared to be 19 inches in length, 8 inches at the ball of the foot, while the heel was 6 inches in breadth. He said the prehistoric human's stride was a little odd, only 2 feet 3 inches, but explained that was most likely due to the fact they were wearing such large wooden sandals. The prints, he concluded, were clearly made by a "pre-Adamite" (before the biblical Adam and Eve) man.

The story generated considerable interest in Carson City's giant prehistoric human footprints. Stories appeared in the *New York Daily Tribune* (August 12, 1883), *Popular Science* magazine (1881), the *San Francisco Chronicle* (September 12, 1881), and other publications. Other scientists who visited the site, however, did not share Harkness's views regarding what type of creature had made the prints. About a year after Harkness's report, Professor Othniel C. Marsh of Yale University suggested that the prints were more likely made by an extinct gigantic ground sloth (*Mylodon robustus*), which can appear to walk on two legs because its hind feet land almost exactly over the prints of its forefeet, a stride that would lengthen the size of the print.

The debate festered for several decades before paleontologist Chester Stock published a scientific paper in 1917 that was specifically designed to settle the issue once and for all. He analyzed the prints and concluded that they were nearly identical to imprints made by giant sloths that he had uncovered at the Rancho Le Brea asphalt pits in Los Angeles. He also studied bone fragments found in the quarry and discovered that some were from a prehistoric giant ground sloth. The evidence, he wrote, "removes still further the possibility that the Carson footprints are to be attributed to a member of the Hominidae [human race]."

The Mint Closes, Opens, and Closes for Good

Despite the fact that the federal government invested half a million dollars to build and equip the U.S. Mint in Carson City, the facility was never a favorite of many members of Congress, particularly Democrats. As a result, during the quarter century that it operated, roughly 1870 to 1893, it was nearly always threatened with being closed. Carson City historian Willa Oldham notes that the mint became "a political football" because whenever the Democrats controlled the federal government they would shut down the mint but when Republicans were in control it would remain open.

For its first eight years, the mint operated without incident. In fact, 1876 was the busiest year in the facility's history; more than 6.4 million coins were produced that year. It seemed that demand for coinage from the mint was only going to increase, so in late 1878, a one-story addition was constructed to house a larger boiler room, an engine room, a storage area, and a carpentry shop. Early the next year, however, there was a change in administration—a new secretary of the U.S. Treasury was named—and the mint's silver coinage operations were curtailed. Forty-eight employees were laid off but rehired five months later. In October 1879, former president Ulysses S. Grant visited the Carson City Mint, which was festooned with red, white, and blue banners, several shields, and flags of many countries. A month later, the mint shut down again, this time because of a lack of bullion. It reopened in May 1880 but was closed for several months in 1881, again because of a lack of precious bullion. It was also at this time that rumors began circulating that some mint workers were "sweating" the gold ingots, meaning they were removing a portion of the gold from the bars and replacing it with a less precious metal such as copper. A U.S. Secret Service special agent was sent to Carson City to investigate the claims and discovered a yeast can containing about $300 in granular gold in the barn of a refinery foreman. The accused man, however, was able to prove he had obtained it legally from another source, so the charges were dropped and the agent returned to Washington. It would not be the last time that the federal government would question the mint's security.

In 1881, the mint was expanded again, with a second floor added to the rear wing of the building for a new refinery. For the next few years, mint operations hummed along at nearly full capacity. In his book, *Mint Mark: "CC": The Story of the United States Mint at Carson City, Nevada,* historian Howard Hickson noted that things began to change with the election of Democrat Grover Cleveland as president in November 1884. "The Republicans in the Carson City Mint (most of the employees were members of the GOP at the time) knew their days were numbered," he wrote. "Gloom shadowed the offices and shops." Not surprisingly, by early 1885, nearly all of the mint employees were fired and the mint was closed down (it continued to serve as an assay office and storage facility for bullion). The following year, 1886, was the first year since the mint had opened that no coins were produced, and all of the bullion was shipped to other mints around the country. While the facility continued to refine silver and gold, no coins were produced in 1887 and 1888.

In November 1888, a pro-silver Democrat, Benjamin Harrison, was elected president and, several months later, ordered the Carson City Mint reopened. In September 1889, the coin presses were again pumping out silver and gold coins. The following year, Carson City installed its first electric streetlights and one was placed on the mint's northwest corner. During the next two years, the mint continued to operate at nearly full capacity.

But in 1892, Grover Cleveland was reelected president and the tug-of-war between those who favored a gold standard and those wanting a two-metal system of gold and silver again commenced. Complicating things for the Carson City Mint was the fact that the Comstock mines were not generating much ore, so there was no longer a need to make coins or refine ore close to the source. In mid-1893, the mint's coin presses were shut down for good. The facility continued to serve as an assay office and refinery but its coin-making days ended.

The mint's ultimate fate was decided with the discovery in 1895 that some employees were sweating gold from the ingots. At the end of 1892, Hirsch Harris, an employee of the melting and refining department found that several gold bars were lighter than they should have been. He reported his findings to a subordinate, John T. Jones, who dismissed it as loss associated with the melting process that would most likely be accounted for in the waste and slag left behind. The shortages, however, continued, so in early 1895, Harris told the mint superintendent, former Nevada governor Jewett W. Adams, who requested an investigation. Andrew Mason, superintendent of the U.S. Assay Office in New York City, was sent to Carson City to study the situation. Mason determined that $75,549.75 in gold was missing, including a small bar of gold and a number of gold ingots that appeared to be their stamped value but actually contained not only gold but a portion of copper and ash. He concluded that the theft had to be an inside job.

Mason's findings triggered a more formal probe, which was followed by arrests. Several former and current employees were charged with stealing from the mint, including Henry Piper, a refinery worker who two years earlier had been found with gold amalgam (an alloy of mercury and gold) in his lunchbox but dumped it down a hoist shaft (he had been fired but not charged with any crime at that time). Others implicated in the crime included John T. Jones, the assistant melter and refiner; James Heney, a former employee who had converted two large bags of nearly pure granular gold into ingots at a Reno reduction works; and William J. Pickler, a mint melter who, it was discovered, had ten pounds of silver and gold amalgam hidden at his home. A grand jury indicted Jones, Heney, and Piper, but Pickler died before he could be charged with anything.

The three indicted men were put on trial in 1895 and 1896. The first defendant, Heney, was found guilty following a second trial (his first ended with a hung jury) and sentenced to eight years in prison and a $5,000 fine. Similarly, Jones was tried twice (again because of a hung jury the first time) and given the same sentence. Piper was found guilty of lesser charges and ordered to pay $300.

As a result of the scandal, mint operations were immediately closed down for a few months but then reopened for the receipt and processing of bullion. The mint limped along for another few years (in 1899, it was formally downgraded to an assay office). Finally, in 1933, the federal government pulled the plug on the entire operation. The grand sandstone building stood dormant until 1939, when it was acquired by the state of Nevada. In 1941, it became home for the Nevada State Museum.

The Spin on Carson City's Ferris Wheel Connection

The man who invented the amusement ride that bears his name—the Ferris wheel—spent much of his childhood in northern Nevada. Born in Galesburg, Illinois, in 1859, George Washington Gale Ferris Jr. was five when his family relocated to a ranch in the Carson Valley, near present-day Minden. His father, George W. G. Ferris Sr., ranched for several years before deciding to relocate to Carson City, where he started a landscaping business. He purchased the Gregory A. Sears house at 311 W. Third Street (still standing and now known as the Sears-Ferris House) and was responsible for planting much of the landscaping in Carson City, including the State Capitol grounds and a giant blue spruce that is now the official state Christmas tree, which he planted in 1876. The senior Ferris also planted trees imported by rail from Illinois around the family house.

George Ferris Jr. spent most of his childhood in Carson City. In 1875, he left Nevada to attend the California Military Academy in Oakland. In 1880, he received his degree in civil engineering from Rensselaer Polytechnic Institute in Troy, New York, and after graduation, he relocated to New York City to design bridges, tunnels, and trestles. Recognizing the growing market for structural steel, he moved to Pittsburgh, the heart of the country's steel industry, and started G. W. G. Ferris & Co., a civil engineering firm that tested and inspected metals for bridges and railways. His company was so successful that he opened offices in New York and Chicago.

In 1891, Ferris attended an engineers' banquet in Chicago, which had just been selected to host the World's Columbian Exposition in 1893 (more commonly called the Chicago World's Fair). The fair's organizers challenged the assembled engineers to create some type of structure that would surpass the Eiffel Tower, which had been built for the 1889 Paris International Exposition.

There are various versions of how Ferris concocted his idea for a giant steel wheel with suspended carriages—the Ferris wheel. According to some, Ferris thought up the design after recalling the waterwheel at Cradlebaugh Bridge on the Carson River, near his father's ranch. Another story is that Ferris was inspired by a giant waterwheel that operated in South Troy, New York, which he no doubt saw while studying near there. Ferris's version to a reporter was that one day he was sitting in a restaurant thinking about ideas for the exposition when, he recalled, "I hit on the idea. I remember remarking that I would build a wheel, a monster. I got some paper and began sketching it out. I fixed the size, determined the construction, the number of cars we would run, the number of people it would hold, what we would charge, the plan of stopping six times in the first revolution and loading, and ten making a complete turn. In short, before the dinner was over, I had sketched out almost the entire detail and my plan never varied an item from that day."

Ferris's concept was to build a steel wheel with a 250-foot diameter rotating on a 45-foot axle that was 82 inches in diameter and weighed 56 tons. Powered by two 1,000-horsepower engines, the wheel would rise 266 feet and carry 36 passenger cars. When completed, the whole contraption would weigh about 4,100 tons.

Despite skepticism from some of his engineering peers, who felt the wheel would collapse under its own weight, Ferris pursued his idea. He spent an estimated $25,000 of his own money on plans and specifications. The fair's board of directors did not initially believe the wheel was feasible but finally gave him the green light, with the condition that he find his own financing for the project.

On June 21, 1893, the Ferris wheel opened for business. While it was seven weeks behind schedule, the ten-minute ride became the most popular attraction at the world's fair, with 1.4 million riders. It easily recouped its $250,000 cost, making about $726,000 (at 50 cents a person) during the fair's nineteen-week run.

Sadly, Ferris gained little from his invention. Smaller versions were built at amusement parks around the country but he didn't receive much in the way of remuneration. Additionally, an attraction patterned after the Chicago Ferris wheel, known as the Great Wheel of London, opened in that city in 1895. It was slightly larger than the original at 270 feet in diameter and could accommodate 1,600 passengers at a time.

According to writer Dennis Bell, Ferris continued working on bigger and more elaborate wheels but found no takers to build them. His obsession with the wheel caused him to neglect his other business. Bell writes, "George's wife finally left him in early 1896 as he slumped deeper into despair and depression." With his firm nearly bankrupt and his personal life in shambles, Ferris moved into a cheap hotel in Pittsburgh. He died alone on November 21, 1896, of typhoid fever. He was thirty-seven years old.

In the years after his death, other giant Ferris wheels opened around the world. In 1897, the 200-foot Riesenrad ("Giant Wheel" in German) opened in Vienna and in 1900, the 300-foot "La Grand Roue" opened in Paris for the Universal Exposition. In 1904, the original wheel was moved to St. Louis for the Louisiana Purchase Exposition. Two years later, it was destroyed for scrap. Today, only the Riesenrad remains of those classic nineteenth-century Ferris wheels.

Carson City: Nevada's Former State Capital?

It is perhaps ironic that one of the men who was most instrumental in locating the state capital in Carson City, Nevada's U.S. senator William Stewart, made an attempt in the late 1880s to move the seat of state government to Winnemucca. Stewart's main concern was that the declining condition of Virginia City's mining industry had thrown Nevada into a severe economic decline, which some thought threatened its status as a state. The production of Comstock mines plummeted from nearly $40 million during the years 1876 and 1877 to slightly more than $1 million by 1881. With the loss in mining production came a steep drop in population. In 1880, Nevada had 62,266 people, but by 1890 the number of residents had declined to 45,761 (and would drop to 42,335 by 1900). The statistics were equally bleak for Carson City. While the number of residents jumped from 3,222 to 5,412 between 1875 and 1880, by 1900 the population had fallen to 2,893—a 47 percent decrease.

Stewart's solution was to annex portions of politically weaker territories such as Idaho and Utah in order to expand Nevada's population and economic base. In 1888, Stewart proposed adding northern Idaho to Washington and southern Idaho to Nevada and suggested Winnemucca as the new capital of the expanded Nevada because of its location in the center of the new state. The proposal was shelved after opposition surfaced from President Grover Cleveland and, not surprisingly, residents of the Idaho Territory. Not willing to drop the matter, Stewart made another attempt at annexation in the summer of 1888. Reasoning that most of southern Idaho's opposition came from the citizens of Boise, he suggested dual capitals of Nevada in Boise and Carson City. Idahoans, however, still preferred statehood and Stewart's proposals died in Congress. In 1890, Idaho was finally admitted as the forty-third state.

The decade between 1890 and 1900 was perhaps the most challenging in the state's young history. The demise of Virginia City's mining industry had virtually shut down the state's most important economic engine. Efforts to shift the state's economy to agriculture and ranching were thwarted by Mother Nature. The "White Winter" of 1889–90 is considered by many weather historians to have been the harshest and most intense period of icy precipitation in state history. By January 1890, temperatures in the Reno–Carson City area were 20 below zero (°F) and the region received more than 51 inches of snow during the four-day period between January 5 and January 8. In northeastern Nevada, temperatures fell to 60 below and resulted in the loss of an estimated 95 percent of all cattle in that part of the state during that winter.

Additionally, a national financial crisis, known as the Panic of 1893, had a severe negative impact on Nevada's economy. The panic was sparked by several factors including a crash in the nation's railroading industry, which had greatly overbuilt in the 1880s. When these railroads began to fail, they dragged down the banks that had loaned them money. The uncertainty triggered a run on the nation's banks by a public that was fearful that its deposits were no longer safe.

Perhaps the most damaging aspect of the panic in regard to Nevada was the repeal that year of the Sherman Silver Purchase Act of 1890, which had required the U.S. Treasury to purchase silver using notes backed by either silver or gold. The act had been extremely popular in western states like Nevada, which produced large quantities of silver. Opponents of the act, which mandated that the federal government purchase 4.5 million ounces of silver bullion monthly, successfully argued that investors, largely from Europe, were buying the silver Treasury notes and redeeming them for gold, which was depleting the country's gold reserves and contributing to the national panic.

In Nevada, the devastating effects of the Panic of 1893 (which lasted for several years) included bank closures, the closing of the U.S. Mint in Carson City, as well as the shutting down of a number of its railroads, most of which primarily served the mining industry, and many of the remaining mines. It would take some ingenuity and a willingness to embrace certain previously unacceptable activities—such as legal prizefighting—for Nevada to begin to turn things around.

The 1897 Corbett-Fitzsimmons Fight

In the latter part of the nineteenth century, most states considered competitive boxing barbaric. By the 1880s, boxing was illegal in every state, although matches were more or less tolerated in a few places. In 1896, New York became the first state to legalize professional prizefighting (four years later, however, it again was made illegal because of fixed fights and several deaths). A year later, Nevada became the second state to legalize the "sweet science" of pugilism. The Nevada Legislature legalized boxing specifically to allow the heavyweight championship bout between James J. "Gentleman Jim" Corbett, the titleholder, and challenger Bob (Robert) Fitzsimmons, the New Zealand champion.

News of the fight's being scheduled incensed religious leaders across the country. On March 9, 1897, Reverend Levi Gilbert of the First Methodist Church of Cleveland was quoted in the *New Haven Evening Register* as proclaiming in a sermon (titled "Nevada's Shame and Disgrace"), "This state[Nevada], this deserted mining camp, revives brutality by an exhibition that must make its Indians and Chinamen wonder at Christianity. . . . [S]uch exhibitions promote criminality by feeding the bestial in man."

Despite the condemnation, on March 17, 1897, Corbett met Fitzsimmons in a wooden arena built for the fight, which was located near what is now the corner of Musser and Harbin streets in Carson City. About six thousand people crowded into the outdoor amphitheater to watch the spectacle between Corbett, a stylish boxer who had defeated the great John L. Sullivan to win the title, and Fitzsimmons, a brawler mostly known for his strength and stamina. Among those in attendance were famed former lawmen Wyatt Earp, reportedly brought in to manage security, and Bat Masterson, a sports writer and columnist for *George's Weekly* in Denver. Others in the crowd included the former champion Sullivan and Nevada's governor, Reinhold Sadler. The fight was noteworthy because it was the first ever filmed for later public exhibition in theaters as well as the first movie ever filmed in Nevada. Additionally, women were permitted at the bout, which was scheduled for forty-five rounds, with the winner receiving $15,000 and the loser getting $9,000.

One of the reporters covering the fight was Nellie Mighels Davis, who became the first female to ever report on a prizefight (she was paid $50 by a Chicago paper to cover it). She took the assignment because her husband was called out of town. She later recalled that she was one of only a handful of women at the fight and nearly all the rest were prostitutes. Because of her concern about propriety, she insisted on using her maiden name (Verrill) on her story.

The fight began with Corbett the aggressor. After bloodying Fitzsimmons in the fifth round with several shots to the head, Corbett dropped Fitzsimmons with a left hook in the next round. The challenger prevented himself from falling to the canvas by grabbing Corbett's waist. The film shows him sliding to the mat until his right knee rested on the floor while he hung on to Corbett's leg. Fearful of being called for a foul, Corbett yelled for referee George Siler to get Fitzsimmons to let go of him. When Fitzsimmons finally released his grip on Corbett, more than fifteen seconds had passed—time during which Fitzsimmons was able to recover from Corbett's blow. This lengthy interlude has become known as the controversial "long count," because Siler didn't begin his knockdown count of Fitzsimmons until after the challenger had relinquished his hold on Corbett. As it was, Fitzsimmons only managed to get to his feet following a nine-count.

Avoiding the loss of the fight in the sixth round, Fitzsimmons began wearing Corbett down. In the thirteenth round, Fitzsimmons rocked his opponent with a solid jab that allegedly knocked one of Corbett's gold teeth into the crowd. During the next round, Fitzsimmons sensed that Corbett was weakening so he feinted with his right to the champion's head, and then when Corbett raised his arms to block, hammered him with a solid punch to the solar plexus (the spot above the stomach and below the heart), which paralyzed Corbett. The champion slumped to the canvas, unable to get up, and helplessly watched as the referee counted to ten.

In addition to being the first championship prizefight held in Nevada—and the beginning of the state's long and successful relationship with professional boxing—the event provided an enormous boost to Carson City and the state of Nevada. Newspapers throughout the country, some of the same papers that had condemned Nevada for allowing the fight, had Carson City, Nev., datelines on their stories. Additionally, the film version of the fight was played in theaters throughout the country and prominently mentioned the name of the city and state that had hosted the event.

Carson's Chinatown

By 1880, Carson City had the largest Chinese population in the state of Nevada, at a time when Nevada ranked third in the nation in Chinese residents, behind California and Oregon. An estimated one thousand Chinese people lived in the capital city, mostly in a five-block area that was located on East Third Street between Fall Street on the west and Valley Street to the east. Today, the Nevada State Printing Office, the Nevada Supreme Court, the Department of Employment, Training & Rehabilitation buildings, and the Legislative Parking Garage have been built over the site. Known as Chinatown, the district had a joss house (a place of worship), a Chinese Masonic lodge, hotels, shops, restaurants, laundries, gambling houses, opium dens, and brothels. According to Arif Dirlik and Malcolm Yeung, editors of *Chinese on the American Frontier,* the colony was nearly self-sufficient and many of the residents—about 90 percent of which were adult males—often worked as laborers, cooks, and launderers for the surrounding non-Chinese population.

Dirlik and Yeung wrote that the Chinese were concentrated in Carson City because they were banned from working and living in nearby Virginia City. Additionally, many had come to the Carson area to work on construction of the Virginia & Truckee Railroad line from Carson City to Virginia City and stayed because there continued to be employ-

Carson City's Chinatown, 1940s. (Special Colletctions, University of Nevada, Reno Libraries)

ment. While for many years the Chinese were tolerated, by the late nineteenth century a rising anti-Chinese immigrant mood had taken root in northern Nevada, including Carson City. In the general election of 1880, Nevadans voted overwhelmingly to abolish further Chinese immigration.

The vote achieved its intended effect; during the next decade the Chinese began leaving the state, including Carson City. Additionally, Nevada's mining industry had fallen into an extended slump, which resulted in a statewide economic depression—and fewer jobs for Chinese workers.

In his book *Back to the Twenties: His Memories of Growing Up in Carson City*, Jack Curran wrote that by the 1920s, "the total population of the old-time Chinese couldn't have been more than forty or fifty (probably less than that), and most were quite elderly. They hadn't married, or had left their spouses behind in the Old Country, so there were few Chinese women in Chinatown (probably not over four or five). The men who could still work were employed around the Arlington Hotel as cooks or dishwashers, and there was a little laundry run by a family on Carson Street."

Curran described the community as "a typical Chinatown in Carson consisting of a lot of shacks, which were pretty well gone by the twenties, along with several substantial stone and brick buildings, which were in reasonably good shape. One of these stone buildings was a Joss House . . . obviously a church or some kind of place for religious ceremonies. Although we had never been witness to what went on in there, we could look in through the unlocked front door and see all the walls and furniture decorated in bright red paper covered with gold Chinese lettering. Several punks would be burning in vases around the room. We never saw any Chinese inside the building, but someone must have come there every day to light the punks."

According to Dirlik and Yeung, Carson City's Chinese population dropped to between twenty and thirty-one residents by the mid-1930s. By then, only two rows of aging wooden buildings remained standing and most were uninhabited. They reported that in 1938, a visitor from San Francisco, Thomas W. Chinn, wrote about his observations concerning Carson City's Chinatown, noting that the surviving structures, such as the Chee Kung Tong building (once the joss house) and the Wui Hsien Low building (a house of prostitution) were proof of the once substantial size and scope of the community. He also talked to the few remaining old-timers still living in the district, all in their seventies, who reminisced about the past, including a 1911 visit by Dr. Sun Yat-sen, a renowned Chinese revolutionary leader. He stopped at the joss house to raise funds for his party's efforts to overthrow the Qing Dynasty and create a republic in China.

By 1950, several fires and years of neglect had taken a toll on the old Chinatown district. All that remained were a handful of residents and about half a dozen buildings, including the Chinese Masonic Hall. Finally, in the 1950s, the State of Nevada purchased the district site with the intention of bulldozing it in order to construct new state office buildings. The last of the dilapidated structures was demolished in the early 1960s. In 2003, the Carson City Preservation Coalition erected a permanent commemorative plaque on the corner of Stewart and Third streets to mark the former site of Chinatown.

Carson City's Historic Ranches:
Gardner, Borda, Nevers-Winters, and Lompa

Given that Carson City's first business was a trading post that sold goods and locally grown crops to travelers heading to California, it's no surprise that agriculture has played an important role in much of the community's history. Among the earliest settlers in Eagle Valley were a number of ranchers and farmers who set down roots in the eastern Sierra, including Dr. Benjamin L. King, who acquired land on the western edge of the valley (at the base of today's King's Canyon area) in 1852, and Matthew Culbertson Gardner, who arrived in Eagle Valley in the early 1860s and, by 1870, had acquired three hundred acres south of the center of Carson City.

Records of the time indicate that Gardner's ranch was one of the valley's largest. In addition to his ranch, Gardner also operated the largest sawmill supplying wood to the Comstock mines. In the early 1870s, he erected an elaborate two-story house near Carson City, which stood until it was destroyed by a fire in 1918. When he died in 1908, the *Carson City News* described him as "a central figure in the logging and lumber industry of the early days, and traces of his work can still be seen from Carson City over the mountains to Tallac." Today, the site of Gardner's home is adjacent to South Carson Street, immediately south of the intersection with Stewart Street. A historic marker in front of a stone building housing the Nevada Division of Forestry marks the location. His ranch spread out in the meadows directly to the southwest.

In 1947, brothers Pete and Raymond "Dutch" Borda purchased a chunk of land at the base of King's Canyon that was once part of Dr. King's holdings. There the brothers established a sheep camp and pastured their flocks in the upper canyon during the summer months. The Bordas also owned a ranch in Dayton, where they would winter their animals. They also often ran sheep in the Pine Nut Mountains [in Douglas County] and Monitor Pass area. When "Dutch" Borda died in 2004, his son, Tom, told the *Nevada Appeal,* "He and his brother (who died in 1996) mostly kept each other going. They were the two toughest guys I ever met." In the late 1990s, the Borda family sold the four-hundred-acre former sheep camp at King's Canyon to the U.S. Forest Service, which maintains a joint management agreement with Carson City for the property. The sale kept the parcel intact and open to the public.

Another pioneering Eagle Valley rancher was Samuel Nevers and his wife, Eliza, who purchased a substantial parcel on the west side of the valley near Ash Canyon in the 1850s. The Nevers had lost their children to

Barn on the Lompa Ranch, 2009. (Richard Moreno)

influenza so they brought a nephew, Ira Lee Winters, to live with them. Winters eventually acquired the Nevers property and later expanded his holdings to include several surrounding ranches. In a 2002 oral history, his son and daughter-in-law, JohnD and Kay Winters, recalled that their property encompassed several hundred acres and once stretched from the end of Robinson Street and was bordered to the south by King Street and to the northeast by the V&T railroad tracks on what is now Washington Street. "We lived at the ranch until 1965, and you can't make a living on subdivision land, and so on," Kay Winters said. "Also we were unable to keep our livestock there anymore because of the dogs in town. One night we lost 47 sheep—just to the dogs. . . . [W]e just got crowded out."

A more recent but still historically significant ranch is the Belli-Lompa Ranch, located south of U.S. 50 near present-day Carson High School. In the early 1900s, a Swiss-Italian immigrant, Steve Belli, acquired the ranch, which dates to the mid-nineteenth century. In 1936, Sam and Eva Lompa purchased the 820-acre parcel and operated a dairy farm and sheep ranch on the property, which still boasts a barn that is said to be more than one hundred years old. According to the *Nevada Appeal,* for many decades the Lompas sold dairy products to a creamery in Minden. When that business closed in the early 1960s, they converted their land into a cattle operation. In the early 1970s, the Lompas donated land for Carson High School (near the intersection of U.S. 50 and Saliman Road). Subsequent land sales, including the sale of 82 acres to the Nevada Department of Transportation in 2004 for a freeway bypass, shrunk the ranch to its present size of about 418 acres. Since 2006, the ranch has been on the market for prospective residential or commercial development with an asking price of $76.6 million. It is the largest parcel of undeveloped private land remaining in Carson City.

The Great Washo Basketmaker

Until Dat So La Lee, handmade baskets were generally viewed as something merely utilitarian. She made them art. Born in the Carson Valley near Woodfords in 1829 or 1830 (although many historians believe she may not have been born until 1850, and the earlier dates were a concoction of later promoters), Dat So La Lee was a member of the Washo tribe. Little is known about her early years except that her birth name

Washo basketmaker Dat So La Lee.
(Nevada Historical Society)

was Dabuda and her father's name was DA DA uongala. In about 1871, she began working as a servant for the Harris Cohn family in the mining camp of Monitor in eastern California. She also was married at least once during those years, including to a man named Assu or "Lame Tom," who is believed to have died of consumption. In 1888, she married again to Charlie Keyser, a part-Washo ranch hand who was at least a decade younger. Keyser had taken his last name from the family that owned the Keyser and Elrod Ranch in the Carson Valley. At that time of her marriage, she took the name Louisa Keyser (the Dat So La Lee name would come later).

Her talent as a basket weaver was not well known until about 1895, when a Carson City merchant, Abe Cohn, bought a handful of willow-covered bottles that she had crafted. Cohn was impressed by the intricate, tightly woven patterns in her work and decided to begin selling her baskets in his emporium. With the help of his wife, Amy, Cohn became Keyser's patron, manager, and publicist. By 1899, he maintained complete records, which were separate from his other business, of every basket she created. A natural promoter, Amy Cohn began naming the baskets and writing brief narratives describing the meaning of the various designs. Some of these scripts were elaborate fairy tales about such things as how, as a young girl, Keyser had met explorer John C. Frémont during his 1844 expedition through Nevada. A copy of her handprint, which was copyrighted, along with information about stitches to the inch, design aspects, and amount of time spent weaving the artwork (some could take as much as a year to finish), was attached to each of the baskets.

It was also about this time that Louisa Keyser became known as Dat So La Lee. As with much of the information about her, there are different stories for how she adopted this name. One of them, told by Abe Cohn, was that it was a nickname that in the Washo language translated as "wide hips." Another was that she took the name to honor Dr. Simeon L. Lee, for whom she had once worked as a maid. Whatever the origin, the Cohns incorporated the melodic name into their marketing efforts.

In return for her creating the baskets and weaving in public to promote the business, the Cohns provided Keyser (who preferred her English name) and her husband with a small rent-free board-and-batten cottage (331 West Proctor) adjacent to their home and paid for their food, clothing, and medical care. Additionally, during the summers the Cohns moved the basketmaker to a shop they operated in Tahoe City at Lake Tahoe. There, she would weave baskets for the Cohns' more well-heeled Tahoe clientele. Keyser also traveled with the Cohns to arts and crafts exhibits and shows, including a major art exhibit in St. Louis.

It is believed that Keyser wove between 120 and 300 baskets during the three decades she worked with the Cohns. Collectors say her work is exceptional because of her precise weaving technique and the unique designs found in her baskets. She is credited with inventing a style called "degikup," which involved starting with a small circular base that extends upward and outward before narrowing to an opening that is nearly the same size around as the base. Her preferred materials were willow, rosebud, and bracken fern.

While in the early 1900s some of her baskets sold for only a few dollars each, they have greatly increased in value over the past century. Today, sales of Dat So La Lee baskets are extremely rare and when one does come up for sale it can command as much as $800,000. In 1978, a thief stole four Dat So La Lee baskets from the Nevada Historical Society in Reno. Two years later, one was returned after the state paid a $2,500 reward. According to an FBI report, the other three turned up in Tucson, Arizona, in 1998 with an art dealer who was attempting to have them appraised by British Columbia art professor Marvin Cohodas to determine their authenticity. The dealer sent photos to the professor, who immediately recognized them as the stolen Dat So La Lee baskets and contacted authorities. Eventually, the state reclaimed the three baskets in return for $55,000, the price the dealer paid for them. No one was ever prosecuted for the crime.

In 1919, Amy Cohn died shortly after returning from an exhibit in St. Louis. Abe Cohn remarried soon after her death but unlike Amy, his second wife, Margaret, had little interest in the business. In 1922, Abe Cohn produced a short film depicting Keyser preparing materials and weaving baskets. She had become so well known that in 1925, noted photographer Edward Curtis had her pose for several portraits for his groundbreaking multivolume work, *The North American Indian.*

Keyser died in 1925 and was buried in the Stewart Indian School cemetery. Charlie Keyser continued to be taken care of by Abe Cohn until Keyser's death three years later. Abe Cohn, who had a large inventory of Dat So La Lee baskets, continued to promote them until his death in 1934. According to Dr. Marvin Cohodas, who has written extensively on Washo basketmakers, including Dat So La Lee, Cohn's death coincided with a decline in interest in Native American curios and collectibles. As a result, Margaret Cohn closed the store in 1937 and, between 1944 and 1945, disposed of the remaining inventory. She sold twenty of the baskets for $1,500 to the state of Nevada. Today, several are displayed at the Nevada Historical Society in Reno and the Nevada State Museum in Carson City.

The Stewart Indian School

The Stewart Indian School in Carson City was founded in 1890 to assimilate Native American children into mainstream American culture. In its first decades, mostly Nevada Paiute, Shoshone, and Washo children were forced to attend the school. Operated much like a military school, the students were prohibited from speaking their native tongues or practicing native customs and rituals.

The roots of the Stewart Indian School can be traced to the 1880s when Nevada Superintendent of Public Instruction Charles S. Young recommended to the U.S. Bureau of Indian Affairs and the Nevada State Legislature that an Indian industrial school be established because most of the state's Native Americans were not being formally educated.

The Nevada State Legislature passed legislation in 1887 that enabled the establishment of an Indian school and authorized the issuing of bonds for the facility, provided the federal government would agree to operate the school. Nevada's U.S. senator William Stewart guided the federal legislation to approval, including congressional funding, and the Clear Creek Indian Training School, as it was originally known, was built by the Bureau of Indian Affairs on 240 acres on what is today Snyder Avenue, south of Carson City.

Later, the school was named for Senator Stewart (it was called a number of names over the years, including the Carson Indian School, the Stewart Institute, and finally the Stewart Indian School), and it officially opened on December 17, 1890.

Records indicate that on opening day, the school had a superintendent (William D. C. Gibson), three teachers, and thirty-seven students from various Nevada tribes. Within a month, additional students were added, bringing the coeducational enrollment to ninety-one by January 1, 1891.

Historic photos show that students wore military-style uniforms. Academic classes were conducted for about half of each day, followed by vocational training with boys learning farming, ranching, blacksmithing, carpentry, shoemaking, and printing while the girls studied dressmaking and cooking.

In 1934, the federal government changed its official policy regarding the school from assimilation to one more tolerant of tribal languages and customs. In later decades, the Bureau of Indian Affairs encouraged students to speak their native languages and to celebrate their distinctive cultures.

Almost from the school's beginning, athletics were a popular aspect of the campus. While relatively small in size, the school managed to win several state championships, including a 1916 state football title, seven consecutive state "AA" cross-country championships in the 1970s, and the

1966 state "A" basketball championship. Additionally, over the years the school's band, which was organized in 1896, performed at parades and events throughout the state and in competitions, including a National Music Festival in Long Beach, California, in 1940. The school was also responsible for producing Nevada's first Native American newspaper, the *Indian Advance*, which was published in 1899.

In addition to educating Nevada's Native Americans (who were actually a minority of those who attended the school by World War II), the Stewart facility housed Native Americans from throughout the country, including children of the Hopi, Apache, Pima, Mohave, Ute, and Tewa tribes. In the late 1940s, the school became part of a special program for Navajos and by the mid-1950s, most of the students were of Navajo descent.

The school was finally closed in 1980, after the federal government decided to phase out Indian boarding schools. The land was sold to the State of Nevada, which has restored many of the buildings for various state offices.

On a visit to the campus, the first thing you notice about the dozens of buildings scattered about is their unique architecture. Built of rough-cut, multicolored native stones quarried from the Carson River and embedded in dark mortar, the walls of the buildings have a quilt-like, patchwork appearance. According to historical reports, the so-called "Stewart Indian School" architecture was a style borrowed in the early 1920s by then-superintendent Frederick Snyder, who had admired a church of similar design in Arizona. The first building of this design (the former Administrative Building, which is still standing directly east of the museum) was completed in 1923. Eventually more than sixty buildings utilizing the stone architecture were constructed on the school grounds, most built by stonemasons trained at the school. Today, visitors can explore or picnic on the school grounds, which are open to the public.

Chapter Four

America's Smallest State Capital

The capitol dome was not much of a dome, but then Carson City was after all the smallest capital in the United States. This was drummed into the children of Carson from day one by townspeople and schoolteachers and the Carson City Daily Appeal. *The children accepted the boast and repeated it to each other as dutifully as if it were one of the Commandments.*

—ROBERT LAXALT, The Basque Hotel

The setting for the 1976 film *The Shootist*, partially filmed in Carson City, was the year 1901. It presented an idealized version of how the city might have appeared at that time. In the film, noteworthy for being John Wayne's last movie, Carson City is depicted as a small frontier city with dirt streets and fine Victorian storefronts and houses. The downtown is built around a square, which surrounds a gazebo. A horse-drawn rail system, called the Carson City Traction, winds through the community. While perhaps accurate for some town during that time, the Carson City presented in the film bears little resemblance to the actual community. Other than several scenes shot on Mountain Street (John Wayne's character, aging gunfighter J. B. Books, who is dying of cancer, stays in the historic Krebs-Peterson House on Mountain) and a scene filmed at Washoe Lake, the majority of the movie was photographed on a studio back lot. Indeed, the Krebs-Peterson House wasn't even built until 1914, and Carson City's horse-drawn trolley to Warm Springs, east of town, only operated in the early 1860s. However, the film's producers named the local paper the *Morning Appeal,* which was the name of Carson City's main newspaper at that time.

Yet despite the historical inaccuracies, in a very broad-brush manner

the film captures many of the cultural and social transitions that were
happening at that time. For instance, scenes where horses are spooked by
a two-seater automobile would have had a basis in reality, as would the
overall theme of the end of the era of frontier lawlessness, represented by
Books's dying, and the spread of "civilization" to the West. *The Shootist*
version of Carson City also has indoor plumbing as well as electricity
and telephones in homes—all of which would have come into existence
in the real community by that time.

Carson City at the beginning of the twentieth century was a quiet
little town. The decline of the Comstock mines had curtailed its role as
a supply point for Virginia City. Coupled with the downgrading of the
Carson City Mint to an assay office in 1899 and a general statewide economic malaise, the city settled into an extended period of general stag-
nation. In 1900, the population was 2,893. The figure rose to 3,415 in 1910,
but then dropped to 2,453 in 1920. The Virginia & Truckee Railroad,
headquartered in Carson City, experienced very little growth during
the early part of the century. In 1903, ore from major mining strikes in

Tonopah and Goldfield was funneled north on the Carson & Colorado Railroad, and then shifted onto the V&T line for the forty-one-mile journey from Mound House to Reno via Carson City. But that mini-boom quickly ended when the C&C, which was owned by the Southern Pacific Railroad, decided it no longer wanted to share its revenues with the V&T; a year later, a fourteen-mile branch line was built from Fallon to Hazen, which was on the main Southern Pacific Railroad line.

Realizing that the Reno to Virginia City route was no longer as lucrative as it was once, the owners of the V&T looked south of Carson City for new business and, in 1906, constructed a fourteen-mile branch from Carson City to Minden. Rail historian David Myrick noted that there were many rumors that the railroad would later extend the Minden line to Bridgeport, California, or the mining boomtown of Aurora, Nevada, but nothing was ever built. During the next decade and a half, the V&T remained profitable as a result of the development of agriculture in the Carson Valley, occasional mining activity in Virginia City, and passenger traffic between Reno and Carson City. However, starting in 1924, the railroad began to lose money. According to Myrick, the V&T recorded deficits for every year between 1924 and 1950, when the railroad was finally shut down.

A Visit from the Hero of San Juan

Perhaps the biggest event to occur in Carson City in the newly birthed twentieth century was a visit to the community by President Theodore Roosevelt on May 19, 1903. The president's train, traveling from California, arrived in Reno very early that morning as part of a cross-country speaking tour. After switching engines, the train continued south to Carson City. Roosevelt arrived at the V&T depot at about 8:45 AM and was transported by carriage to the State Capitol. Speaking from the front of the building before an estimated crowd of some 7,000 (at the time the city's entire population was about 3,400), the president spoke for about a half hour, mostly praising the recently passed federal reclamation law, which funded the construction of dams and canals to bring water to dry lands in the West. This law was particularly important in northern Nevada because it included building the Truckee Canal, part of the Truckee-Carson (Newlands) Project, designed to transport water to

the Fallon area for farming. "The opportunities for the development of Nevada are very great," he said. "Until recently Nevada was only thought of as a mineral and stock-raising state . . . but now under the stimulus of irrigation it is probable that irrigated agriculture will come to the front, and when it does the population will increase with a rapidity and permanence never before known."

After his speech in Carson City, Roosevelt reboarded his train and returned to Reno for two brief appearances. He spoke for about fifteen minutes in front of the Washoe County Courthouse and then made a stop at the University of Nevada campus. By 12:30 PM, the presidential train was steaming out of Reno, heading back to California.

Roosevelt's focus on reclamation reflected the popular hope at the time—that Nevada's economy could be lifted from the boom and bust cycles of mining by fully exploiting its agricultural potential. Promoters of the ambitious Newlands Project, constructed between 1903 and 1915, predicted that its 104 miles of canals, 504 miles of laterals, and 335 miles of open ditches (all of which were linked with the 100,000-acre Lahontan Reservoir) would irrigate more than 400,000 acres and give birth to an agricultural district that could support the state. The estimates, however, proved wildly optimistic. Only about 70,000 acres were ever irrigated by the project. Fallon became known as Nevada's breadbasket but never produced the quantity of crops that many thought it would.

Fortunately, another series of mining booms helped pull the state from its two-decade-long economic malaise. In May 1900, large deposits of silver were uncovered in the central Nevada community of Tonopah, and two years later a significant gold strike was made in Goldfield, located about twenty-seven miles to the south. Additionally, large deposits of copper had been uncovered in remote eastern Nevada, near Ely. By 1907, Goldfield had grown to be the largest community in the state, with approximately 25,000 residents, while Tonopah boasted more than 8,000 people. Not surprisingly, some Goldfield boosters proposed relocating the state capital from Carson City to their thriving community in 1909 but the bill died in the legislature. The uptick in Nevada's mining industry provided a slight boost to Carson City, which, as the seat of government, benefited from increased state revenues. This improved state of affairs allowed the state to expand the Capitol building twice; an octagonal annex was built to the rear of the building in 1906 to house the state library and, in 1914, the north and south wings of the building were expanded to provide additional office space and chambers for the assembly and senate.

Carson's High Schools

Carson City's secondary education system can be traced to 1872 and the opening of the all-grades Central School on the corner of Minnesota and Telegraph streets. In 1906, that structure was replaced by the second Central School on the corner of Musser and Division streets, which also incorporated grades one through twelve (grades one through eight downstairs, the upper grades upstairs). By 1937, the school had become too small for the number of students and was split into two facilities: the primary grades remained at the old school while the secondary school classes moved to a larger building, called Carson High School, on Thompson Street.

This second building also became too small after only two decades and was replaced in 1956 by a new $400,000 high school at 1140 West King Street, which was located on land donated by longtime local rancher JohnD Winters. At the time, school officials were criticized for building

Carson City's second Central School, ca. 1916. (Nevada State Archives)

on a site that was thought to be so far out of town. Less than two decades later, however, school district officials were forced to look for yet another, larger site because the King Street high school building was no longer adequate for the growing number of students. In the early 1970s, the King Street high school building was converted into the Carson Junior High School while a new, much larger high school was constructed on the east side of the community at Saliman Road and U.S. 50. Both facilities have been modernized and expanded in subsequent years.

In 1960, the Central School building was sold to the First Methodist Church, which intended to convert it into Sunday school facilities. The structure, however, proved to be too expensive to remodel and repair, so in the early 1970s the church had it demolished. A 1971 *Nevada Appeal* article noted, "the old Carson High School building is posing a monstrous problem not only for its owner but for the surrounding neighborhood. Officials of the First Methodist Church . . . now concede that the church landed a white elephant when it bought it in 1960 for $27,500."

The Governor's Mansion

During the first four decades of statehood, Nevada did not provide a formal place for its chief executives to live. From 1864 to 1909, each of the state's governors either purchased or built a dwelling in Carson City or rented quarters. In 1907, State Assembly Bill 10 (known as the

"Mansion Bill") was passed; it directed the state to finally secure a site and erect a permanent residence for Nevada's governors and their families. Lawmakers appropriated $40,000 for building and furnishing the home. Mrs. Thomas B. Rickey sold a parcel at 600 N. Mountain Street to the state for the token amount of $10, and Reno architect George A. Ferris (no relation to former Carson City resident George Washington Gale Ferris Jr., the man who invented the Ferris wheel) was contracted to design the house.

Ferris produced plans for a two-story, twenty-three-room home with a large grand entry area, a formal dining room, a pair of salons, a private den, upstairs bedrooms, and a large kitchen area. A porch supported by fluted Ionic columns wrapped around the second story. The home's exterior incorporated a Classical Revival style with Georgian and Jeffersonian motifs. Construction began in 1908 and continued until early 1909. According to architectural historian Julie Nicoletta, author of *Buildings of Nevada*, the result was a home with "a sense of formality and grandeur that is seen in few buildings in the state's capital."

The first chief executive to occupy the house was Lieutenant and Acting Governor Denver S. Dickerson, along with his family. His wife, Una, gave birth to a daughter, June, in the mansion on September 2, 1909; she is

The Governor's Mansion, 2008. (Richard Moreno)

the only child ever born in the mansion. Acting Governor Dickerson opened the mansion to the public for the first time on New Year's Day, 1910—a precursor to the modern tradition of opening the mansion to the public each Nevada Day.

During the past century, the mansion has been renovated several times, including a partial refurbishing in 1959, a more substantial remodeling in 1967, and a $5 million reconstruction in 1999–2000, which was funded by private donations. During that most recent remodeling, a 6,608-square-foot addition was built north of the mansion, called the Nevada Room, with a commercial kitchen and meeting space for up to three hundred people. The mansion has hosted seventeen governors and their families since it was built.

A Time of Props and Pistons

The early twentieth century was a time of technological innovation as well as exploration and adventure, all of which managed to touch Carson City. For example, in the summer of 1909, Alice Huyler Ramsey, a twenty-two-year-old Vassar graduate, became the first woman to drive across the United States. Traveling in a Maxwell DA auto with three female companions, Ramsey made the trek from New York to San Francisco in fifty-nine days. Her journey—a publicity stunt sponsored by the Maxwell-Briscoe Automobile Company to show that "even" a woman could drive a car—included an overnight stay at the Riverside Hotel in Reno, then a brief stop and lunch in Carson City. In her 1961 memoir of the trip, *Veil, Duster, and Tire Iron,* Ramsey recalled driving south and confronting the Carson Range and the Sierra Nevada west of Carson City. "The Sierra range confronted us with sudden steepness as we started the climb to its crest soon after leaving the capital. The road was heavy with sand. This was in truth no automobile highway. It was an old wagon trail over the mountains and the grades were stiff. Traffic was largely trucking wagons and powerful horses, mules and even oxen— sometimes just men in the saddle," she wrote.

Shortly after Ramsey's visit, which attracted good news coverage, another barnstorming adventurer, William Ivy Baldwin, was invited to Carson City to fly his home-built, 48-horsepower, Curtis pusher-type biplane for the community's Independence Day celebration in 1910.

The local Sagebrush Carnival Committee had asked him to conduct a trial flight followed by a series of exhibition flights on July 3, 4, and 5 at the Carson City racetrack. The flight attracted national interest because the diminutive Baldwin was a well-known daredevil—he frequently ascended in hot-air balloons and then spectacularly parachuted to the ground—and no one had ever attempted a flight at Carson City's high altitude, 4,675 feet. On June 23, 1910, the 5-foot, 3-inch Baldwin climbed into his aircraft, which was parked on the Raycraft Ranch (located northwest of Carson City, off today's U.S. 395 near West College Parkway), revved up the engine, and guided his plane along a makeshift dirt runway. Within minutes, the airplane had lifted from the ground and begun to climb. Baldwin was able to pilot the little craft to about fifty feet high and a half mile in distance before touching down. This trial was the first air flight in Nevada, and history had been made.

But advances in the air weren't the only kind of changes that came to Carson City at that time. Less than a year after Baldwin's flight, several miles of Carson City's main boulevard, Carson Street, were paved to provide a smoother ride—no doubt Ramsey would have approved— for the handful of horseless carriages that had begun to crop up in the community. Automobiles had become so prevalent that the state began issuing license registration plates in 1913. In the same year, the Lincoln Highway was established as the nation's first transcontinental highway. Across Nevada, the route largely followed the path of today's U.S. 50, except it split into two roads, one from Fallon to Reno and the other from Fallon to Carson City. The two routes were connected by a highway between Reno and Carson City. Travelers made their way into California via Kings Canyon west of Carson City until the route was relocated to Clear Creek Canyon in 1928. In addition to creating an interconnecting series of roadways across the country, the Lincoln Highway Association (formed to promote the road) published several road guidebooks that were packed with useful information for pioneering travelers. For example, the 1924 edition of *A Complete Official Road Guide of the Lincoln Highway* described Carson City as "beautifully laid out and claims the distinction of having more shade and fruit trees than any other city in the state." Additionally, the guide noted that while modern activity "has supplanted the easy life of the past, there is still an air of romance to be found in the city." It noted that Carson Street was paved the entire length of the city, making it one of the finest roads in the West.

In 1919, Carson City was the scene of two additional transportation-related events. On March 22, 1919, the community hosted the first trans-Sierra airplane flight. On that morning, four U.S. Army aircraft (three Liberty-powered DeHaviland aircraft and a 90-horsepower Curtis trainer) landed on an improvised landing strip in a field three miles east of Carson City (near today's Carson High School). The flyers, led by Lt. Col. Henry L. Watson, had taken off from Mather Field in Sacramento, California, and flown over the Sierra Nevada to Carson City. Nevada governor Emmet Boyle greeted the pilots when they landed and agreed to accompany them during their return flight—making him the first civilian to cross the Sierra by airplane.

Later that year, a convoy of seventy-two U.S. Army vehicles arrived in Carson City as part of an exercise to survey the nation's roads and prove the feasibility of transporting military machines and men from one coast to the other. The motorcade departed from Washington, D.C., on July 7, 1919, with the goal of making the 3,200-mile journey in less than two months. Led by Lt. Col. Charles W. McClure of the Motor Transport Corps, the group contained some 280 officers and enlisted men, including an observer, Captain Dwight D. Eisenhower.

For much of the route, the convoy followed the path of the Lincoln Highway. It arrived in Ely on August 21 and stayed in Eureka, Austin, and Fallon before reaching Carson City on the evening of Saturday, August 30. Between Fallon and Carson City, the convoy took the route of the present U.S. 50 west of Fallon past the Lahontan Reservoir and through Dayton. According to Nevada historian Phillip I. Earl, who has written about the trip, several trucks became stuck in sand between Fallon and Carson City, which delayed the group for several hours. Finally, at about 4 PM, the parade of vehicles began arriving in the capital city. "The last of the men got in just after midnight," Earl wrote. "The Carson City Band had played for a street dance earlier in the evening, but most men were too tired to take part and the bandsmen had taken their leave before the last of the convoy had gotten in."

Lt. Col. McClure declared that the next day, Sunday, would be a day of rest and a number of the men were escorted to the Carson Hot Springs for a bath. Earl noted that small groups of the other men were given tours of the community, visiting the prison farm, the Stewart Indian School, the site of the 1897 Corbett-Fitzsimmons fight, and the Governor's Mansion. The convoy resumed its journey the following morning, heading up to Lake Tahoe via steep King's Canyon Road. They concluded their coast-to-coast cruise in San Francisco on September 6.

"A Very Small Place"

As the decade of the 1920s began, Nevada—and by extension, its capital, Carson City—had begun to slide once again into another slump. The boom times in Tonopah and Goldfield were over and while mining continued to be productive, particularly in Ely, few new discoveries were forthcoming. Compounding the situation, on March 24, 1909, Governor Dickerson had signed legislation that outlawed gambling in Nevada (the law took effect the following year). The issue had been contentious since the time of Nevada's founding; women's groups and moral reformers had pushed hard for a sustained ban for decades. In the Fall 1985 issue of the *Nevada Historical Society Quarterly,* historian Phillip I. Earl outlined the history of efforts to control legal gambling that led to the 1909 ban. He said that when the state's economic conditions were good, such as during a prolonged mining boom, the call to end legal gambling grew louder, but when the economy soured the public was more willing to tolerate it. He said that as Reno grew in prominence and size during the beginning of the twentieth century, there was a renewed cry to stamp out the sins of gambling.

"The faculty of the Nevada State College [now the University of Nevada, Reno] had never been reconciled to the notion of legalized gambling, nor had many clergymen, clubwomen and newspapers editors," Earl wrote. "Other opponents included some businessmen and other citizens whose livelihoods did not depend directly upon gambling, the saloon trade, or prostitution."

Not surprisingly, saloonkeepers, gambling hall operators, and hotel owners in Reno and Las Vegas immediately sought to reinstate legalized games of chance (although they wouldn't completely succeed until 1931). In many cases, the legal casinos were simply replaced by illegal games. Corrupt law enforcement authorities were bribed to look the other way.

The Herman Lee Ensign National Humane Alliance Fountain, located across Carson Street from the State Capitol, was donated in 1909 to Carson City to provide water for "men, horses and dogs." (Richard Moreno)

"As many Nevadans predicted, the law outlawing gambling led to the establishment of games in backrooms, basements, and private homes," Earl wrote. Proponents of the ban had argued that eliminating legal gambling would reduce crime by removing the criminal element that surrounded the games. The reality was that, like Prohibition, it ultimately resulted in an increase in crime and corruption.

By 1920, Carson City had lost about a third of its population from a decade earlier and seemed like it would never have to relinquish its title as the country's smallest capital city. In his book *Back to the Twenties,* Jack Curran, who moved to Carson City in 1918, recalled that "Carson [in the 1920s] was a very small place in those days, probably 1800 people or less. Everybody knew everybody else or they seemed to know all about each other. It was quite a town for gossiping and prying into each other's affairs."

According to Curran, Carson Street was where most of the city's action happened, particularly around the large granite fountain across from the State Capitol, erected by the National Humane Alliance. Water poured out of small bronze lion heads with open mouths into an upper bowl for passing horses and mules, while at the base was a lower trough that offered water to dogs and cats. National Guardsmen drilled in the area and someone always seemed to be going by, traveling from one place to another.

Carson Street seemed to me to be an almost continuous parade. Character after character would be slowly walking by, including quite a few "Old Gentlemen" with their bent topped canes, gold watch fobs and chains, and the symbols of their lodges showing. They always seemed to be putting forth their best side for the social approval of their peers; politely doffing their hats to the ladies, (a bit more elaborately than absolutely necessary), while passing along some pleasant words to their acquaintances, always showing their veneration for womankind by their manners.

The ordinary citizens went about their businesses, greeting each other politely or raucously as the occasion demanded, but with never a word of loud profanity, lest the ladies be offended. A few Indians moseyed along a little slower than the rest of the strollers, mostly ignoring the white population, keeping their conversations to themselves, probably laughing a little inside at the posturing white people, who long ago forgot how to be themselves.

Carson's Government Complex Begins to Take Shape

By 1920, Nevada was more than a half-century old and the state's government agencies, as well as Carson City's, were outgrowing their nineteenth-century quarters. In 1919, Reno architect Frederic DeLongchamps, who had designed the 1915 additions to the State Capitol, was appointed the official Nevada State Architect (the only person ever to hold that position) and embarked on a program to design a capitol complex adjacent to the Capitol. The first two structures he designed were the Heroes Memorial Building (to house the state's industrial commission, highway department, and state engineer) and its twin, the Ormsby County

The Ormsby County Courthouse, 1940s. (Special Collections, University of Nevada, Reno Libraries)

Courthouse. Both buildings were Neoclassical in design with large porticos supported by massive columns. Heroes Memorial, which the legislature wanted "designed to be a fitting memorial to Nevada soldiers who gave their lives in the service of the United States in the European war [World War I]" was built at a cost of $80,000 and completed in 1921.

According to Ronald M. James, author of *Temples of Justice,* the Ormsby County Courthouse was an exact duplicate of the war memorial building. "In fact, the plans for the courthouse reveal the title, 'Ormsby County Court House' printed over 'Heroes Memorial,'" James wrote. The courthouse, however, had a substantially different interior from its doppelganger because it contained four jail cells and courtrooms rather than offices. Construction of the courthouse, which cost $65,735 (the county eliminated some features in the original design to cut costs), was completed in March 1922.

A Financial Turn for the Worse

A scandal that unfolded in 1927 rocked the foundations of Nevada state government in Carson City. The case involved State Treasurer Ed Malley, the former state controller George A. Cole, and H. C. Clapp, cashier of the Carson Valley Bank, who conspired to embezzle $516,322.16 in state funds between 1919 and 1926. The three men invested the money in oil company stock, which, unfortunately, did not perform well. Both Malley and Cole were elected treasurer and controller, respectively, in 1914 but Cole lost his bid for reelection in 1926. During that year, Clapp was fired from his bank and agreed to turn state's evidence against his cocon-spirators (he was sent to prison in 1927). Following a widely publicized trial, both Malley and Cole were convicted and sentenced to serve three years in the Nevada State Prison in Carson City. The three men were all released in 1931.

The loss of such a large amount of money was a serious matter for a small state like Nevada. The Nevada Surety and Bonding Company held Malley's bond, meaning that under normal circumstances it was financial liable for his actions. However, George Wingfield, a Reno-based businessman and political power broker with whom many of the state's politicians were allied, owned both Nevada Surety and Carson

Valley Bank. Fearful of a bank run and cognizant of public appearances, Wingfield deposited $500,000 in the bank to prevent its collapse. He then requested that Governor Fred Balzar convene a special session of the Nevada State Legislature to resolve the matter. In his letter to Balzar, Wingfield described both the state and his bank as innocent victims in the Malley-Cole swindle. He did not address his other company's responsibility as the bonding agency for Malley.

In January 1928, the Legislature met to discuss the situation. Wingfield noted the Carson Valley Bank did not have sufficient capital—excluding his deposit—to pay back the half-million dollars that had been stolen. He offered a compromise: he would pay the state $124,000 in cash for release of all bondsmen and to settle any claims the state had against his bank. In his book, *History of Nevada*, Russell R. Elliott also noted that when it was suggested Wingfield might withdraw his $500,000 deposit and prevent collection from the bank, the banker said, in a prepared statement, "I have personally deposited in the Carson Valley Bank the full amount of the money involved, to be there held to meet and liqui-date whatever liability may be legally imposed on the bank." He guar-anteed the people of the state that he would make up for any shortages owed by the bank using his personal funds.

Apparently satisfied that Wingfield had made a good faith effort to be responsible for the whole amount of the money, the legislature agreed to a compromise amount of $154,896.65 to settle the claim. Additionally, a state tax was passed to cover the remainder of the loss, about $360,000, as well as the cost of conducting the special session, the audits, and attor-neys' fees (about $52,000).

By the late 1920s, Nevada's economic engine had once again begun to sputter. The momentum the state had achieved as a result of the Tonopah and Goldfield mining boom during the previous two decades had long since faded, and the country was just about to be slammed by the stock market crash in October 1929 and the Great Depression. The national economic spiral didn't immediately hit Carson City and northern Nevada, but by the early 1930s Nevadans were feeling the effects.

According to former Nevada state archivist Guy Louis Rocha, Nevada was somewhat immune from the economic hardships in the rest of the country because of its remoteness and small population, and "federal highway dollars and public works projects coupled with a thriving migratory divorce industry initially insulated the state from the economic disaster."

By the 1930 U.S. Census, Carson City's population had dropped to 2,221—about as many people as had lived in the city when Nevada had been founded sixty-six years earlier. In their book, *The Silver Short Line: A History of the Virginia & Truckee Railroad,* authors Ted Wurm and Harre Demoro noted, "Carson City [of the 1930s] was a slow town resting under tall shade trees, clean and tidy in spite of dirt streets and occasional horses and farm animals."

Searching for a Golden Goose

The 1931 legislative session in Carson City began with state officials optimistic about the state's ability to weather the economic tsunami sweeping the rest of the country. Congress had approved millions of dollars to fund the Boulder Canyon Project (Hoover Dam), which promised to provide thousands of jobs to southern Nevada, and the federal government made significant expenditures constructing and operating the Hawthorne Ammunition Depot in Mineral County. Additionally, as a result of a generous federal highway program, under which Nevada contributed only a fraction of the cost of construction, there was a steady stream of funding for road building. The state had also received a one-time fiscal bonanza in 1929 when the federal government paid $600 million to settle a half-century-old claim for monies that Nevada had loaned to Washington during the Civil War. Mining, however, had declined again—1930 production was half that of the previous year—and the national economic slide seemed to be growing worse.

Perhaps with all of that in mind, legislators were receptive to a few homegrown ideas that could boost Nevada's burgeoning tourism trade —specifically, liberalizing the state's divorce laws even further to maintain Nevada's role as the leading state to dissolve a marriage, and re-introducing legal gambling. Freshman assemblyman Phil Tobin of Winnemucca, who introduced the legislation to remove the ban on gambling, later said, "The damn state was broke and we needed the money." He added that his motivation for introducing the bill was "there was not a market, hotel or gas station that didn't have a slot machine or two. They were in the old Golden Hotel lobby, and places like the Bank Club in Reno operated openly with casino gambling."

Tobin said he was tired of local law enforcement officials getting paid to look the other way. "The sheriff had the say in who operated a game, and determining who operated a game depended on how much money the sheriff got," he said. "I didn't really give a damn about gambling and I certainly didn't know much about it but I felt that if we legalized it, the tax revenue would be beneficial to the state."

Once Tobin introduced his bill, it quickly gained approval in both houses of the legislature. At nearly the same time, legislators approved a measure lowering the legal residency requirement for a divorce in Nevada to six weeks from three months. According to historian Russell Elliott, the action was taken because the divorce trade had become big business in Nevada, and Arkansas and Idaho recently had dropped their residency requirement to three months to compete against the Silver State. Governor Balzar signed both bills into law on March 19, 1931. Elliott noted that the divorce bill was of more immediate importance to the state's economy, although the gambling bill would eventually prove far more significant. In the 1930s, the already-established easy divorce business generated several million dollars in revenue each year, while gambling wouldn't gain traction for many more years.

Banking Woes

Despite the generally rosy outlook—in 1931, Governor Balzar bragged the state was in excellent shape—about a year later Nevada found it was not entirely immune to the financial crisis gripping the nation. On November 1, 1932, Acting Governor Morley Griswold announced a two-week bank holiday. The action was designed to stall a run on the state's banks, several of which, it was discovered, had insufficient cash reserves. The crisis primarily affected the twelve-bank chain owned by George Wingfield, who apparently had overextended credit to many ranchers and stockmen. Additionally, the state had not properly audited Wingfield's banks for many years. The failure of Wingfield's financial institutions would have a serious impact on the entire state because his dozen banks, located in nine cities, held more than 65 percent of the

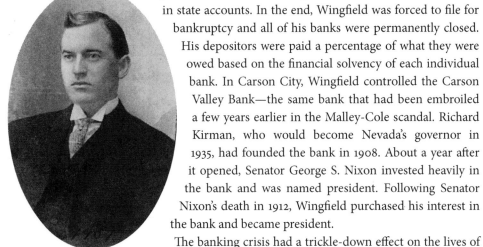

deposits in the state, including more than a half-million dollars in state accounts. In the end, Wingfield was forced to file for bankruptcy and all of his banks were permanently closed. His depositors were paid a percentage of what they were owed based on the financial solvency of each individual bank. In Carson City, Wingfield controlled the Carson Valley Bank—the same bank that had been embroiled a few years earlier in the Malley-Cole scandal. Richard Kirman, who would become Nevada's governor in 1935, had founded the bank in 1908. About a year after it opened, Senator George S. Nixon invested heavily in the bank and was named president. Following Senator Nixon's death in 1912, Wingfield purchased his interest in the bank and became president.

George Wingfield, ca. 1908. (Nevada Historical Society)

The banking crisis had a trickle-down effect on the lives of many Nevadans, not only those who lost their deposits. Among those hurt most were the state's farmers, cattle and sheep ranchers, and stockmen who did business with Wingfield's banks and found they couldn't repay their loans and were unable to find new lines of credit. As a result, many of them also went bankrupt and their properties or assets were sold. Elliott noted that "most farmers and livestockmen in Nevada suffered extreme hardship in the period from 1930 to 1934." Fortunately, Nevada's powerful U.S. senator Key Pittman was able to procure a generous portion of federal assistance funds during the Great Depression. According to Guy Louis Rocha, "Nevada received the highest per capita federal dollars among the forty-eight states benefiting from President Franklin Roosevelt's New Deal programs."

Capital City Improvements

By the early 1930s, it had become obvious that the tiny Nevada Supreme Court chambers at the State Capitol were inadequate for the court's needs. The court originally occupied leased space in the Great Basin Hotel and then was moved into the Capitol when it was completed in 1871. For about six decades, the three-member court met in a small second-floor courtroom that contained almost no office space for the justices or their clerks. In 1935, the legislature appropriated $160,000

to construct a new home for the Supreme Court and the State Library (which had also outgrown its quarters in the Capitol) on a Carson Street site between the Heroes Memorial Building and the Ormsby County Courthouse. The same architect who had designed those two structures, Frederic DeLongchamps, was called upon to design the new court building. This time, DeLongchamps incorporated a sleek, modern, Art Deco style that was significantly different from its Neoclassical neighbors. When it opened on September 13, 1937, the 21,000-square-foot building served as home for the Supreme Court and its staff as well as for the Attorney General and the State Library.

The last of the major public works completed in the capital city in the late 1930s was the Carson City Civic Auditorium, finished in 1939. This elegant red-brick auditorium, located a block north of the Virginia & Truckee Railroad Depot on Carson Street, was designed by Reno architect George A. Ferris, who had also designed the Governor's Mansion. The building was designed as a multi-use facility that could host stage plays, performances, public meetings, community dances, and basketball games.

By the 1960s, the Civic Auditorium had become too small a venue for many community events and there was a push to build a new, larger facility to host theatrical performances, convention groups, and pub-

The Carson City Civic Auditorium, 1998.
(Richard Moreno)

lic meetings. During the next several decades, the Civic Auditorium was used as a temporary City Hall as well as the first home of the Ormsby County Library. In the mid-1990s, the venerable structure gained new purpose when the city leased it to the nonprofit Children's Museum of Northern Nevada for a new hands-on children's learning and discovery museum. Using state and federal grants, the museum renovated the building interior, replaced the roof, and installed an elevator.

The Birth of Carson's Nevada Day Parade

The Nevada Day Parade event was the inspiration of a Reno advertising executive, Thomas C. Wilson, and Judge Clark J. Guild of Carson City. While there had been small celebrations in Reno in previous years, Wilson and Guild wanted to create an annual celebration in the capital city that would properly commemorate Nevada's state admission day, which is October 31. Working with local service organizations including the Carson City Rotary, the Carson City Lions' Club, and the Carson City 20–30 Club, they organized the parade in 1938, featuring dozens of floats, marching bands, and other entertainment. "So well pleased were the visitors from many parts of the state that demands that the annual celebration be a fixture in the state's capital city were heard from every side and quarter," reported the *Nevada Daily Appeal*.

The following year, the celebration was expanded to three days for the state's seventy-fifth anniversary (Diamond Jubilee) and the event attracted an estimated 42,000 visitors. Since then, the Nevada Day Parade has been held annually in Carson City, with the exception of three years during World War II. From 1938 to 1999, the parade was generally held on October 31 (the actual admission day) unless it was a Sunday, in which case it would be moved to the previous Saturday (although there were exceptions: the parade was held on Monday, November 1, 1948, and Sunday, October 31, 1965). The official date of the celebration was

changed by voters in 1998 (an advisory vote) and the State Legislature in 1999 so that beginning in 2000, Nevada Day would be observed on the last Friday in October of each year, with the parade held on the following Saturday.

The Nevada State Museum

As Nevada marked its seventy-fifth birthday, it began to recognize the importance of preserving and studying its past. Once again it was Judge Guild who was instrumental in creating a permanent showplace for the state's rich history and heritage. "In the early summer of 1938, on a Sunday morning, I was taking my usual walk up to the post office for the mail," he recalled in a 1967 oral history interview. "On this particular morning, I went a little further up the street to the old Mint building, and I discovered a sign on the building, 'For Sale.' Well, it rather upset me and bothered me, and I walked back to the group of people standing and sitting in front of the Arlington Hotel. Bill Maxwell was the proprietor. And I said, 'Bill, they're going to sell the old Mint building.'

"He said, 'Well, Judge, do you want to buy it?'

"I said, 'No, I can't buy it, but it ought to never be sold. It would make a wonderful museum.' "

In 1939, Judge Guild persuaded the State Legislature to allocate funds to purchase from the federal government the old Mint, which had been vacant since 1933, for use as a state museum. Between 1939 and 1941, the state used Works Progress Administration assistance and private donations to remodel and retrofit the building for its new purpose. Guild also sought help from private donors to renovate the structure, among them "Major" Max C. Fleischmann, former president of the Fleischmann Company (maker of yeast and yeast by-products), who had established a residence at Glenbrook, Nevada, for tax reasons. Fleischmann became a major donor to the museum during the next few years, providing funds for building rehabilitation, exhibits, and acquisitions.

On Nevada Day of 1941, the Nevada State Museum opened its doors for the first time. A report to the museum's directors noted that five thousand people toured the building on its opening day. "The building is worthy of every praise in its present condition," the report noted. "It places the State Museum in a position to procure, house, and properly display worthwhile 'State' exhibits for many years to come."

Carson Turns the Corner

By 1940, Carson City's population had edged higher, to 3,209 residents—a reversal of the trend during the previous few decades. Among those new residents were James and Thelma Calhoun, who arrived in Carson City that year from Virginia City. In his 1987 oral history, James Calhoun, who served as director of the Nevada State Museum from 1950 to 1973, described it as a quiet town of about 3,000 and noted, "Carson City never knew the Great Depression, because most everyone worked for the state. State government had to go on, and the stores sold to those people who remained. When the legislature was in town, there was a legal limit to the length of the session. When they had to run over (I think 60 days), they would put a cardboard over the clock. Most bills were passed the last legal day, even if it was a week long."

During this period, the city's governing system was revamped to allow for direct election of the mayor. In previous years, the council member elected as the chairman of the city council was referred to as the council president or, after 1916, the mayor. In 1941, C. B. Austin was elected to a two-year term as mayor. He would go on to serve a four-year term because city elections were not held in 1943 due to the Second World War. Carson City's other mayors during the decade included George Lind (1945–47), R. M. Elston (1947–49), and Caro Pendergraft (1949–51).

Like it did on the rest of the country, World War II had a significant impact on the community. Many local young men enlisted in the armed forces and, sadly, a number of them lost their lives; it's estimated that at least eleven young men from Carson City died during the war. In his book, *A Private War*, Robert Laxalt provided a glimpse of how Carson City residents were affected by the war:

> In the days before the war, nothing much distinguished my home town of Carson City from a thousand other small towns scattered across the United States. Generations came and went, children were born, the old died, summers were hot and languid. Then the war came, and all of that was ended. The war caught the town unawares. Except for the college-bound, most grown men had never been out of sight of Carson City. [Now] Carson City males suddenly found themselves scattered around the globe.

The war years were particularly hard on Carson City's few Japanese-American families. Ida Fukui Weiss, who was a teenager during that time, later recalled, "We were still sort of restricted. We couldn't leave and go some place without approval. You couldn't move around as freely,

A look down Carson Street, 1940s. (Special Collections, University of Nevada, Reno Libraries)

but there were people in Carson that I grew up with that were very kind, and they would sign, saying, 'We will vouch for this person. They can go to Reno or wherever.'"

During the war, a Tacoma-class patrol frigate (PF-50) was named in honor of Carson City. The vessel was built at the Consolidated Steel Corporation shipyards in Wilmington, California, and launched on November 13, 1943. Mayor C. B. Austin was on hand to address the officers and crew while his wife officially christened the new ship, which was designated for action in the Pacific. The USS *Carson City,* which had a crew of 182, served as an escort ship in several battles, including the Morotai landings in eastern Indonesia, a preliminary to the invasion of the Philippines, and as part of the Northern Attack Force that fought in the Leyte Gulf. The crew was awarded the Battle Star for its participation in both campaigns. After the war, the ship was decommissioned and leased to the Soviet Navy for four years. In 1949, the *Carson City* was reconditioned and transferred to the Japanese Maritime Self-Defense Force (and renamed the *Sakura,* which is Japanese for "cherry blossom tree") in 1953. In 1971, the ship was decommissioned and returned to U.S. custody, declared surplus, and sold for scrap.

The immediate postwar period, however, is generally recognized as when Carson City began its transition from the sleepy smallest-capital-in-America to a modern, medium-sized community. During his one term in office, Mayor Caro Pendergraft presided over the community when it acquired the land for Mills Park and saw the opening of the Carson-Tahoe Hospital. In a 2008 *Nevada Appeal* interview, Pendergraft said his biggest accomplishment was convincing the Mills family, former owners of the Virginia & Truckee Railroad, to donate the land for Mills Park to the city. The fifty-two-acre site, located adjacent to William Street (U.S. 50) east of the downtown, was formerly an oil storage center for the railroad. Pendergraft said the family agreed to transfer ownership of the land for $10 after he promised the park would carry the Mills family name. "That sold it," he said.

The opening of the Carson-Tahoe Hospital was a particularly important milestone for community members, who had previously had to travel to Reno for any type of serious or complicated medical procedure.

In her book *Carson-Tahoe Hospital: The Story of a Caring Community*, history writer Willa Oldham wrote, "In the 1940s, a ground swell from the residents began in Carson City to express a need for a local hospital." She said the handful of local doctors began agitating for construction of a medical facility. One of those who recognized the need was Major Max C. Fleischmann, whose Glenbrook home was adjacent to the vacation home of Dr. James Thom of Carson City.

> One evening, while the Thoms were entertaining the Fleischmanns, Thom was called out on a case and the Major was also called out to an accident. On the return of the two men, the conversation led to a discussion of the lack of a hospital in Carson City.
>
> Fleischmann put up his hand to gain the attention of everyone. "If you'll get your businessmen to donate, I'll match every dime they give. We'll get a hospital for Carson City," Fleischmann stated.

Following several years of intense fundraising efforts on behalf of the community, the $80,000, eighteen-bed hospital officially opened on May 2, 1949. The first patient was Robert Clark, an employee of the Nevada State Highway Department, who had cracked a kneecap after falling off his horse. Interviewed in the *Nevada Appeal*, Clark noted, "You don't get that whiff of ether that you get in most hospitals. The food is very fine and the service is swell. Carson City can be proud of it."

The following year, 1950, marked not only the start of a new decade but also the end of one of Carson City's oldest and most beloved enterprises—the Virginia & Truckee Railroad. On May 11, 1950, the "Queen of the Short Lines" took one last official, scheduled run between Minden and Reno. After eighty years, the railroad that was founded to carry rich silver and gold ore from Virginia City had shut down (it was officially abandoned on May 31). The closure was no surprise because the line had lost money for several years and had gradually reduced service (the run between Carson City and Virginia City was abandoned in 1938) and started selling off its equipment. Rail historians note that the train made at least one other run between Carson and Reno, including a trip on November 2, 1950, to haul the remains of Locomotive #26 to be scrapped (it had been severely damaged in a fire on May 1, 1950). Newspapers from the day carried the headline "V&T's Last Train" and noted that people along the route were surprised to see the old railroad running again. A short time later, the rails between Carson City and Reno were torn up and sold. An era had ended.

Wungnema House

On the eastern edge of Mills Park, across from Carson High School, is a small stone cottage surrounded by a black iron fence. Known as the Wungnema House, the home was constructed in 1948 by local builder and craftsman Burton Wungnema, assisted by his wife, Pearl, and his father, Earnest. Since work began on the 1,200-square-foot home just after World War II, Wungnema found building materials, such as lumber, nails, and glass, in scarce supply. As a result, he utilized a variety of types of stone from his father's nearby quarries—the reason for the house's distinctive mosaic-like appearance. Additionally, the house's windows were originally destined for several churches at Lake Tahoe, on which Wungnema and his father were working (the two did noteworthy masonry work on many of the homes and churches built around Lake Tahoe in the 1950s). Wungnema was able to purchase the windows because they were made of clear glass—the churches had wanted frosted windows—and were going to be returned to the manufacturer.

The interior of the house was unique. For instance, the fireplace, made of rock imported from Arizona, is faced with stones that were cut into the shapes of clouds and lightning, the symbol of the Water clan of the Hopi Nation. Both Wungnema and his wife, who had met in Carson City and married in 1947, were members of the Hopi tribe. In 1956, Burton Wungnema died at the age of twenty-nine and was buried in the Stewart Indian School Cemetery. His wife lived in the home for many more years, raising their eight children. She died in 2001 at the age of seventy-five.

By the 1980s, the Wungnema House was no longer being lived in and had begun to deteriorate—it was so decrepit that for many years the local Kiwanis Club used it as a haunted house at Halloween. In 1999, the city spent $280,000 to completely restore the aging residence for use as office and meeting space.

Chapter Five

Main Street USA

A tourist motoring south from Reno on U.S. 395 comes to this pleasant little town after a drive of about thirty miles. Carson City is the smallest state capital of any of the forty-eight states. . . . [T]oday, Carson City has begun to gain some attention as a vacation center. —New York Times, *December 30, 1956*

*C*arson City lost its designation as the nation's smallest state capital in 1963 when the city surpassed Montpelier, Vermont, in population. In fact, the Carson City Chamber of Commerce—far more interested in growth and development than in colorful, quaint, and ultimately meaningless slogans—promoted the fact. Losing the status of being the smallest capital, however, was an evolutionary process that had begun in the previous decade, when Carson City finally began to expand after decades of contracting.

The enormous growth in southern Nevada after World War II created unprecedented demand for new state and local services. Clark County's population grew from 48,289 in 1940 to 127,016 in 1960. As the center of state government, Carson City experienced a smaller but still substantial rate of growth in the size and number of agencies necessary to administer to the state's needs. The community's population nearly tripled between 1940 and 1960, from 3,209 to 8,063. To keep up with these demands, state officials embarked on a new capital improvement program that resulted in the construction of several large office buildings in Carson City.

A 1951 *Nevada Appeal* editorial noted:

[That] more and more people are building homes in this community —some of whom have been long-time residents here and others who are newcomers—was evident in a report issued last week by the city clerk's office. His figures showed that the estimated cost of new building, alterations and repairs in Carson City during the year just ended amounted to a third of a million dollars. . . . The fact that Carson is a mighty good place in which to live well might be elaborated upon by the chamber of commerce during the present year. New homes and people not only aid those in the building and construction industry but other business establishments as well.

The 1950s

The first new state building erected since the 1930s was a functional, albeit unattractive, rectangular structure completed in 1951 that was called simply the State Office Building. The $800,000, three-story concrete-and-brick building, located at 201 South Fall Street, originally served as the home of the Nevada Department of Highways (now known as the Nevada Department of Transportation), Nevada *Highways and Parks Magazine* (now called *Nevada Magazine*), and the Nevada Highway Patrol.

In the mid-1950s, the Nevada State Public Works Board unveiled an ambitious master plan to modernize the Capitol Complex. Without a doubt the most controversial element of the plan was to raze the historic State Capitol Building and replace it with a quartet of office buildings surrounding a central quad. On December 30, 1956, the *New York Times* reported, "The venerable building has been inspected by structural engineers and they have recommended its demolition." The newspaper added that the engineers described the building as "something of a firetrap and in the event of a mild earthquake, a not altogether unlikely occurrence in this area, it might collapse." The concerns were real; a series of quakes in the Fallon area in 1954 had caused masonry to fall from the Capitol Building's ceiling.

In 1957, the board actually built the first phase of its plan—the boxy "new" State Office Building on the northeast corner of the Capitol Complex grounds. The structure was erected unusually close to the northern wing of the old Capitol Building because the board assumed it would be demolished. Like the 1951 State Office Building, the 1957 edition was a sturdy but bland concrete-and-glass rectangular three-story building with little architectural charm.

Following the completion of the second State Office Building, many state employees informally referred to the older structure as either the "old" State Office Building or the State Highway Building. In 1964, the State Division of Buildings and Grounds decided to clear up any confusion over the two building names by proposing that they be named after former governors. The original State Office Building became the Nye Building, in honor of James Warren Nye, Nevada's only territorial governor, while the second State Office Building was renamed the Blasdel Building, after Henry Goode Blasdel, Nevada's first elected governor.

The plan to remove the Capitol, however, proved unpopular with most legislators as well as many members of the general public. In 1959, the Nevada State Assembly passed a resolution formally calling for the old Capitol to be preserved and restored rather than destroyed.

Another old building that gained new life was the venerable Carson Brewery on the corner of King and Division streets, which had closed in 1948. Three years later, the eighty-seven-year-old structure was renovated and became home of the *Nevada Appeal* newspaper. In addition to the newspaper's business and editorial offices, the former brewery building housed the newspaper's production and distribution facilities as well as its large printing press. Initially, the *Appeal* used the same press that it had in its previous home. The late Bill Dolan, who wrote the column "Past Pages," which appeared in the *Appeal* for fifty-nine years, once noted that printing was labor-intensive because the press could print only one side of a page at a time and the pages had to be turned over so the other side could be printed. Fortunately, the old single-sheet press was replaced about a month after the move into the brewery building with a duplex, roll-fed, high-speed press that was far more efficient.

The 1950s in Carson City were a time of rapid growth as the community nearly doubled from 4,172 residents to 8,063 (finally surpassing the size it had been in 1880, when the town had a population of 5,412). A 1956 *Nevada Appeal* editorial proclaimed, "We who live in Carson City are proud of it, happy to work for it, and firm believers in its future. But sometimes we're so close to it that we don't realize just how well it is progressing. Many state legislators have commented this year on how much improvement and growth they note in Nevada's capital city in just the few months since the last session."

The state of Nevada was also experiencing a sharp increase in population, ballooning from 161,145 in 1950 to 287,660 in 1960. In 1954, the small Carson Nugget casino opened adjacent to the historic Federal Building on North Carson Street, reflecting the growing economic importance of legal gambling on Nevada's economy in the post–World War II era. The Nugget's original owner, Richard Graves, later said he wasn't sure if Carson was large enough to support the modest casino (originally the entire operation was about the size of the current Nugget coffee shop) when it opened. "The Carson Nugget took right off," he said in a 1978 oral history. "It was very surprising to me because Carson was a sleepy little town. There wasn't much business in town." In the August 4, 1954, issue of the *Nevada Appeal,* Graves says that business had been "terrific" and he was already working on the second addition to the club since the opening five months earlier.

Graves, who also opened Nugget casinos in Sparks, Yerington, and Reno, added a coffee shop, which was managed by John Ascuaga (who

Billboard for the Carson Nugget, ca. 1955. (Special Collections, University of Nevada, Reno Libraries)

became a very successful casino-hotel operator after purchasing the Sparks Nugget from Graves in 1960). In 1957, Graves sold the Carson Nugget to Hop and Howard Adams, who greatly expanded the facility after buying the adjacent buildings all the way to the corner of Carson and Robinson streets. As part of that reconstruction, the Adams brothers added a duplicate of the famous Las Vegas Golden Nugget neon sign (ironically, the Golden Nugget original is now gone, the victim of progress). In 1982, the Adams brothers added a second story to the casino and expanded the property to encompass more than 80,000 square feet. Howard Adams died in 1999 and his brother continued managing the business until his death in 2003. In 2008, the Adams family, which had continued to own and operate the property, announced plans to sell it to an unnamed developer, who would convert the casino into a nonprofit corporation benefiting Carson City charities. Under the proposal, the Adamses would continue to manage the casino.

The Nugget wasn't Carson City's only casino. In the late 1930s, the Senator Bar had opened on North Carson Street and offered a limited number of slot machines and other games. In 1968, the property was expanded, renovated, and renamed Mike's Senator Club. At that time, the casino also erected a two-story neon-trimmed animated sign depicting a cartoonish Old West–style politician, known as the Senator. As in the iconic neon cowboy sign "Vegas Vic," in downtown Las Vegas, the mustachioed senator's arm moves up and down as he waves a "Howdy" buck in his hand. (In 2007, the Senator sign, which has become a Carson City landmark, was spiffed up—the character's yellow suit was cleaned and his neon was replaced.)

In 1971, Peter "Cactus Pete" Piersanti, who had earlier founded the town of Jackpot on the Nevada-Idaho border (where he established Cactus Pete's Hotel and Casino) purchased the Senator and renamed it Cactus Jack's Senator Club. Piersanti operated the casino and restaurant, which primarily appealed to locals, until his retirement in 1989. He died in 1994. In recent years, the 9,400-square-foot casino and restaurant has been owned by a succession of regional gaming investment companies.

While not quite as old as the Nugget, the Silver Spur Casino opened south of the Senator Bar in 1955. Like the Nugget and the Senator Bar, it offered rows of slot machines and a handful of table games. Housed in a historic brick structure that was built in the late nineteenth century, the Silver Spur closed in 1973, only to reopen two years later with a new name, the Lucky Spur. The 10,000-square-foot casino closed again in 1978 and the building sat vacant for the next twenty-seven years. In 2005, with the help of a $100,000 redevelopment grant from the city, the former casino was substantially renovated and converted into a brew pub–sports bar called Stew's. The business, however, struggled and in 2007 it was sold to a new group of investors, who rebranded the place and rechristened it Doppelgangers Brewery.

The 1960s

The statewide election of 1958 resulted in a sea change in Nevada state government with the victory of Democrat Grant Sawyer for governor. Not quite forty years old, Sawyer was different from the men who had previously served in that position. In his oral history, Sawyer noted that his campaign literature "featured a photograph of me striding forward, one foot boldly out in front of the other, a glow around me. I had a crew cut. That projected the image of a young man on the move—vigorous, in contrast to what we were alleging to be an administration that was asleep at the switch and not doing anything."

Two years later, when U.S. senator John F. Kennedy of Massachusetts—another up-and-coming young political figure—was running for president, he campaigned in Carson City with Governor Sawyer's support. On January 31, 1960, less than a month after declaring his candidacy, Kennedy stood on the stage of the Carson City Civic Auditorium and briefly addressed a crowd of local residents. A day later, he spoke to a joint session of the Nevada State Legislature in the State Capitol and attended a reception at the Governor's Mansion. In his oral history, *Hang Tough!: Grant Sawyer, An Activist in the Governor's Mansion,* Governor Sawyer recalled that Senator Kennedy and his press aide, Pierre Salinger, took a drive to see Lake Tahoe before arriving at the mansion. "We weren't sure exactly when to expect them, but they arrived at the governor's mansion a couple of hours before

Governor Grant Sawyer with Senator John F. Kennedy in the Governor's Mansion, 1960. (Nevada State Archives)

the reception was slated to begin. [First Lady] Bette [Sawyer] met them at the door," Governor Sawyer said. "Bette had curlers in her hair, and she was terribly embarrassed and completely surprised, but they came in and made themselves at home.

"I was taking a shower when Bette came upstairs and said, 'Senator Kennedy is here.' I said, 'Well, tell him to come in.' He came in and sat on the toilet while I finished my shower, and we talked a little. Then he changed his clothes and I got ready for the reception," Sawyer continued. "There were literally hundreds of people from throughout the state lined up in front of the mansion waiting to get in." About a week after Senator Kennedy's appearance, another U.S. senator running for president also addressed the State Legislature. On February 9, 1960, Minnesota's senator Hubert H. Humphrey, who would later be elected vice president under President Lyndon Johnson, stopped by the Capitol and shared with lawmakers his vision for the country.

More State Building

The early 1960s saw the construction of two new state office buildings: a new Nevada Highway Department facility, which opened in 1965, and a new Department of Motor Vehicles building, which was completed that same year. The Highway Department building on South Stewart Street contained more than 100,000 square feet of office space and, according to former state highway engineer W. Otis Wright, "this additional room will make it possible for us to provide improved highway services to meet the growing demands of Nevada and the motoring public." Built at a cost of $3.2 million, the four-story building had a red-brick veneer and room for the 425 staff members of the highway department. The Department of Motor Vehicles building, built adjacent to the Highway Department building on South Stewart, was a bit more modest with 31,500 square feet of office space. The two-story structure cost about $750,000 and also boasted red-brick exterior walls. Both buildings were later expanded, the Highway Department (later called the Nevada Department of Transportation) in 1977 and 1994, and the DMV in 1980.

A July 1963 issue of *The Nevadan,* the Sunday magazine of the *Las Vegas Review-Journal,* described Carson City as "Nevada's Lovely Little Capital." Author Bob Richards, a former editor of Virginia City's *Territorial Enterprise* and one of the fathers of the Virginia City Camel Races, noted with some hyperbole that "there are those who come to Nevada's capital at this warm and verdant time of year to declare that in appearance it is a transplant from New England; quiet, tree lined streets; elderly dignified homes; an unhurried atmosphere that reminds them of towns that were old many years before Carson City was a gleam in the redoubtable Abe Curry's eye."

That nostalgic image, however, didn't completely reflect the reality. From 1960 to 1970, Carson City's population jumped from 8,063 to 15,468. As the community grew, so did the need for new and better services. In 1965, the Nevada State Library stopped allowing Carson City residents to borrow books from its shelves. The practice had been in place since the 1890s, and over the years hundreds of Carson City children had grown to depend on the library for their reading needs. In his autobiography, author Robert Laxalt noted, "In the years of my growing up in tiny Carson City, the Nevada State Library was my second home. . . . [T]he Nevada State Library, of course, was dominated by books dealing with the history, people, and economics of the state. It was almost too much to expect that the library would contain a considerable wealth of books for the general public, but ours did."

The state's decision forced city leaders to confront the fact that the community had relied for too long on the state for such a basic community service. Almost immediately after the state library was closed to local residents, Ormsby County commissioners created the first board of trustees for an Ormsby County Library. In 1966, a small community library opened in the basement of the former Civic Auditorium with shelves of donated books and publications loaned by the state library.

Within three years it became obvious that the basement did not provide adequate space for the growing library's number of patrons and rapidly growing collection. In 1970, the trustees obtained funding from the Fleischmann Foundation, which was supplemented by federal grants, to construct a new facility. Later that year, construction started on a 13,500-square-foot structure on the corner of North Roop and East Washington streets. It officially opened on May 10, 1971. About a decade later, the library again found itself growing out of its facility and the trustees obtained a second Fleischmann Foundation grant to finance an 8,000-square-foot addition, which was completed in 1980.

The late 1960s also saw the building of a new $2.5 million Carson-Tahoe Hospital. Despite expansion of the hospital in 1959, by the mid-1960s it had become clear that the facility, operated by the nonprofit Carson-Tahoe Hospital Corporation, was too small for the needs of Carson City but didn't have the resources to grow. In November 1964, voters approved transferring ownership of the hospital from the Carson-Tahoe Hospital Corporation to Ormsby County. The change allowed the county to seek voter approval to sell bonds to finance the construction of a new hospital. On July 11, 1967, groundbreaking ceremonies took place for the new facility.

On August 26, 1968, while the new hospital was under construction, the old hospital building was seriously damaged in a fire. A later investigation concluded that the fire had been started when a workman on the new hospital building had carelessly placed excelsior (dense wood shavings used as packing material) into a fire he had started in order to destroy boxes and other trash from the construction site. Apparently, the wind picked up a smoldering piece of the wood material and carried it to the roof of the old hospital, where it became jammed in the eaves and eventually caused a fire to break out.

Fortunately, all of the hospital's patients and staff were safely evacuated from the facility once the fire had started. The building, however, was nearly a total loss (in December, it was bulldozed). Despite efforts to accelerate construction of the new hospital, work wasn't completed until November 10, 1968. In the three-month interim, Carson City residents could visit a temporary emergency room at the Carson Medical Center across Mountain Street or travel to Reno for major medical care. The *Nevada Appeal*, however, noted in the headline of a special twelve-page supplement devoted to the hospital's opening that the new health care center was "Worth Waiting For."

The newspaper added, "The atmosphere was as festive as a hospital is likely to get, an elderly couple holding hands and children peering into a delivery room bassinet in search of babies, still unborn. Candystripers, Pink Ladies and other volunteers were on hand to point out everything from the most sophisticated equipment to a flower festooned bedpan." An estimated three thousand people turned out for the grand opening, most taking a seventy-five-minute tour of the new hospital, which boasted a $50,000 computerized X-ray room as well as state-of-the-art heart monitoring equipment. Hospital historian Willa Oldham wrote, "All of these new facilities and equipment made Carson-Tahoe Hospital a far cry from what was available in 'the little old hospital.'"

BY THE LATE 1950S, it had also become obvious that one of the city's most iconic buildings, the 1891 federal courthouse/post office building, was inadequate for the growing community's needs. The federal court, jammed into a single courtroom and a handful of offices, required new quarters, and the equally crowded post office, located on the first floor, also required more space. Officials, led by Postmaster Wilford Dunfield, pushed for construction of a new, much larger federal building. In 1962, the federal government began looking for both a new federal office site and a post office. Ultimately, the government decided to relocate the federal court and offices to Reno—a blow to Carson City's prestige—and construct a new post office in Carson City.

On September 21, 1970, the new Carson City Post Office opened in a sprawling, tan-colored brick building on East Washington Street between Plaza and Stewart streets. The 18,515-square-foot facility boasted considerably more space and a modern loading dock, and it housed a handful of other federal agencies such as the Bureau of Indian Affairs. A pamphlet distributed at the building's dedication noted, "It is equipped with the most modern equipment that the Post Office Department has at its disposal at this time."

The community also found itself in a position to develop new parklands for its citizens. In the 1860s, the Ormsby County Poor Farm had been established at the south edge of Eagle Valley on Old Clear Creek Road for those unable to find work and an affordable place to live. Less-fortunate citizens could live in a dormitory-like building erected on the banks of Clear Creek and work on the farm, earning a few dollars.

The poor farm operated for about a century before it was replaced by other social programs (its last few residents were placed in local nursing homes). In 1965, the county was gifted with $20,000 by Basil Woon, a British-born author (*When It's Cocktail Time in Cuba*), playwright (*Misdeal*), and screenwriter, who had retired in Carson City. Woon donated the money with the caveat that it be used for a public park named in memory of his wife, Fuji.

County supervisors decided the former poor farm site would make an ideal public park and formed a Fuji Park Committee to oversee the project. Over time, the fourteen-acre Fuji Park complex evolved into a mixed-use facility that includes a grassy, shaded park section with picnic tables, benches, a playground area, and a one-acre urban fishing pond (fed by Clear Creek, which opened in 2010) as well as the Carson City Fairgrounds. The latter includes a rodeo arena, grandstands, a sixty-stall barn, a small open-air animal barn, and an indoor exhibit hall.

The only reminder of the site's original use as a poor farm is a tiny, half-hidden cemetery on the park's southeastern edge that contains two headstones encircled by a black iron fence. The graveyard is the final resting place for two military veterans, John Thoroughman and James Johnson. Thoroughman, who was born in 1838 in Ohio, enlisted in the army in Dayton, Nevada, in June 1863, was inducted at Fort Churchill, Nevada, and served for three years. He died in 1909. Johnson, also born in Ohio (Cuyahoga County), enlisted in the army in March 1865 from Marysville, California, and served in the 4th Regimental Cavalry Infantry Volunteers. He died in 1910.

In addition to a new library, hospital, post office, and park, the 1960s saw the paving of most of the city's side streets for the first time. While a portion of Carson Street in the downtown had been paved in 1911, many of the city's roads remained graded dirt or gravel into the middle of the twentieth century. According to former Nevada state archivist Guy Rocha, it was during Mayor James Y. Robertson's tenure (1963–69) that most of the capital city's streets were finally paved. Additionally, Mayor Robertson, who owned a local furniture store, led the effort to move parking off downtown Carson Street, thereby widening the road for traffic, and, in 1964, approved the city's first enclosed shopping mall, the three-acre Carson Mall at the intersection of South Carson and

South Stewart streets. The $3 million mall, which opened in March 1966, included a 60,000-square-foot Gray Reid department store, a Safeway store, Bobby Page's Dry Cleaners, Carson Travel, Marge's Yarn & Fabric Shop, and Swensen's Ice Cream. The mall was touted in the *Nevada Appeal* as "one of the most complete shopping centers in all of Nevada, virtually all types of merchandise can be obtained with a minimum of inconvenience."

Ormsby County Is No More

No doubt the most significant change in Carson City's government occurred in 1969 when Carson City and Ormsby County were consolidated into one government entity. The consolidation recognized that Carson City had grown so much that it virtually encompassed most of the county's population. The Ormsby County communities of Lakeview and Empire City had ceased to exist and many taxpayers questioned the need for two layers of government for such a relatively small area (155.7 square miles, the smallest of all the state's seventeen counties).

The consolidation effort had its detractors. On October 27, 1968, the *Nevada Appeal* reported that former Carson City mayor Al Autrand (1961–63) appeared in a public forum on consolidation and attacked the proposed change as well as the public officials supporting it. According to the *Appeal*, Autrand accused the city and county of already having started the process of consolidating their operations "illegally" and wondered why city and county officials "were trying to push this thing down people's throats."

However, with the support of nearly every elected city, county, and state official, as well as the *Nevada Appeal,* many other newspapers across the state, and most local business groups, voters statewide approved the merger (called Proposition #3) by a margin of 73,913 to 42,541 on November 5, 1968. During the legislative session that immediately followed the election, the State Legislature approved a city charter that took effect on April 1, 1969. Under the terms of the charter, the consolidated city-county of Carson City is led by an elected mayor and a four-member board of supervisors. The mayor and the supervisors are responsible for making policy decisions, while a professional city manager and city staff, who are hired by the Board, implement those policies.

Consolidated Carson City's first city manager was Henry Etchemendy, who also has the distinction of being the last county manager of Ormsby County. Etchemendy as well as Mayor Robertson and former Ormsby County chairman William Goni are often credited with ushering in the community's new era of consolidated government. In a 2008 *Reno Gazette-Journal* interview, Goni, who was a sheep rancher at Tahoe Meadows for many years, remembered there was considerable enmity between city and county officials during his eighteen years on the board. He noted that one time the Carson City Police Department and the Ormsby County Sheriff's Department began to publicly squabble during a city council meeting because a city police car had crossed into the county—and there were other arguments over which entity had the authority to use certain equipment and employees. Reporter Sue Morrow, a longtime observer of Carson City politics, wrote,

> Goni well remembers the dual, and sometimes dueling, government entities at the time when Carson City had a city council and Ormsby County had a county commission. There was a city police department and a county sheriff's department and other duplicitous [*sic*] city and county departments.
>
> So it was with unrestrained enthusiasm that he recalled the years-long effort toward the consolidation of the City of Carson City and Ormsby County that went into effect on July 1, 1969. After earlier mayors rebuffed the idea, Mayor Jim Robertson, elected in 1963 and retained in 1967, was receptive to consolidation. Goni credits Robertson for being the impetus for helping himself and others get the plan approved and implemented.

The Laxalt Family and Carson City

Perhaps no family is as identified with Carson City in the latter part of the twentieth century as the Laxalts. Dominique and Therese Laxalt moved to Carson City in 1926. Dominique Laxalt had been in the sheep business since arriving in America in 1906 from the Basque province of Soule, France (located in the Pyrenees, which border Spain and France). When he arrived, Dominique was nineteen or twenty years old, homesick, knew no English, and had a limited education. Despite the hardships, over the next decade and a half, he was able to build a successful sheep and cattle operation in Nevada and California. By 1921, Dominique was a part owner of the Allied Land and Livestock Company, which not only owned several large herds of sheep and cattle but also raised crops on five ranches and farms. That year, he married Therese Alpetche in Reno. Therese was born in the French Basque province of Basse Navarre. She graduated from Le Cordon Bleu in Paris and, following World War I, traveled to the U.S. to assist her brother, Michel, who was being treated for poison gas that he had inhaled as a soldier in the French army during the war. Michel died in Reno in 1920 and his sister decided to stay in America.

About a year after their marriage, the Laxalts suffered a serious financial setback. A statewide livestock crash wiped out Dominique's company and he was forced to take the remainder of his sheep to northern Washoe County in order to start over. Unfortunately, a particularly harsh winter that year caused him to lose nearly all the rest of his livestock. The result was that Dominique and Therese spent the next few years wandering through northern California and Nevada as he worked as a sheepherder and ranch hand at various outfits. During this time, she often worked as a ranch cook, preparing meals three times a day for as many as thirty men.

Dominique and Therese Laxalt had six children, all of whom were extraordinarily successful in their careers. The oldest, Paul (b. 1922), was elected Nevada's governor in 1966 and then served two terms in the U.S. Senate (1974–1986). Robert (b. 1923) was the founding director of the University of Nevada Press and author of seventeen books, including the classic *Sweet Promised Land,* which related his father's bittersweet trip back to his Basque homeland after being gone for nearly a half century. Both John (b. 1926) and Peter (b. 1931) had long and successful careers as attorneys. Marie (b. 1928) was a schoolteacher for many years, while Suzanne (b. 1925) became a Roman Catholic nun with the Holy Family order.

In 1926, the Laxalts purchased the French Hotel in Carson City. Son Robert later described it as a "little boardinghouse hotel of four bedrooms, a dining room and a saloon." He said his mother had scraped together $100 for a down payment. Robert said his mother's fine cooking attracted some guests, but the family quickly realized the only way to compete with other local lodging houses was to offer, as the other places did, whiskey and wine (this was during Prohibition). "I suppose this made us bootleggers, but hardly in the league of Al Capone and Joe Kennedy, who operated in grand style with fleets of trucks loaded with Scotch whiskey instead of poor man's bourbon," he wrote in his autobiography, *Travels with My Royal*.

A few years later, Dominique Laxalt tired of town living and returned to raising sheep in the hills above Carson City as well as near Dayton and above Lake Tahoe and in Washoe Valley. Paul Laxalt recalled in his memoirs that "as time passed, [my father] felt increasingly trapped. Inside life simply wasn't for him." Therese leased the French Hotel to another Basque couple and, in 1931, purchased the Ormsby House, the venerable but crumbling Carson City landmark on the southwest corner of Second and Carson streets that had been erected in 1859 by Major William Ormsby and enlarged and rebuilt several times over the years. Finding the building virtually uninhabitable, she had it demolished and later sold the site.

In 1935, the Laxalts purchased a historic house at 402 N. Minnesota Street that had been built in 1872 by local lumber baron Duane L. Bliss and later owned by Theodore R. Hofer, superintendent of the U.S. Mint. According to Paul Laxalt, the house had a large living room and dining room but lacked enough bedrooms for all of the children. "Mom solved the problem by having a screen porch attached to the back of the house. This became a dorm of sort for us four boys. Great in the summer, but a killer in the winter," he said.

In a 2008 interview with *Nevada Magazine,* Paul Laxalt recalled the Carson City of his youth: "We had a couple thousand people at best. It was an exercise in simplicity in every way. Only one street in Carson City was paved, and that was the main street. That was good because we not only didn't have much traffic, but Sundays were reserved for bike racing, which we would have from the front of the Capitol to our little [French] Hotel on Carson Street. We went to school in a building where we had all 12 grades, and our home was in walking distance of school and church."

In 1950, Paul Laxalt was elected district attorney for Ormsby County (Carson City). He served one term before returning to private practice. In 1962, he was persuaded to return to politics and was elected lieutenant governor. Two years later, he unsuccessfully ran for the U.S. Senate, losing by forty-eight votes to incumbent senator Howard Cannon. In 1966, he became Nevada's twenty-second governor. He temporarily retired from politics after a single term in the Governor's Mansion and in 1972 joined his brother Peter to open a new Ormsby House hotel-casino in Carson City. Named after the historic property once owned by his parents, the new two-hundred-room Ormsby, located three blocks south of the site of the original, was ten stories high—making it the tallest building in Carson City (it remains so). While the hotel provided Carson City with some much-needed first-class accommodations, it was not a financial success. In 1975, the Laxalt group sold it to veteran casino operator Woody Loftin.

Paul Laxalt returned to politics in 1974, when he was elected to the U.S. Senate from Nevada. He was reelected in 1980, the same year that his close friend, former California governor Ronald Reagan, won the presidency. During the 1980 Republican National Convention, Paul Laxalt's name was floated as a potential vice presidential candidate on the Reagan ticket (George H. W. Bush was selected instead). In 1987, he decided not to seek a third term in the Senate and made a brief run for the Republican Party presidential nomination, which was won by Vice

Governor Paul Laxalt, along with former first lady Jacqueline Laxalt and two of his children pose with California governor Ronald Reagan and his wife, Nancy, at Lake Tahoe, 1967. (Nevada State Archives)

President George H. W. Bush. After leaving the Senate, he became a Washington lobbyist and opened his own firm, the Paul Laxalt Group.

Robert Laxalt had equally impressive success as a journalist and as a man of letters. After graduating from the University of Nevada in Reno, Robert started the Capital News Service and provided stories about state government to several daily newspapers throughout the state, the *Sacramento Bee* in California, and the United Press bureau in Reno before becoming a staff correspondent for United Press Associations. Faced with being relocated by the wire service to another state, Robert quit daily journalism in 1954 and was hired as director of news and publications by the University of Nevada. In 1957, Robert published *Sweet Promised Land,* for which he gained national attention. From 1961 to 1983, he was director of the University of Nevada Press, which he helped to found. From the mid-1970s until his death in 2001, Robert Laxalt was not only a prolific writer but also a popular journalism instructor at UNR. In 1988, he was named the first Distinguished Nevada Author Chair at the university and was inducted into the Nevada Writers Hall of Fame. His best-known books include *A Man in the Wheatfield* (1964), *A Cup of Tea in Pamplona* (1985), and his autobiographical Basque trilogy, *The Basque Hotel* (1989), *Child of the Holy Ghost* (1992), and *The Governor's Mansion* (1994).

Robert Laxalt, 1993. (Nevada Historical Society)

As for Dominique Laxalt, he retired in 1947 but soon returned to the hills with his sheep, where he would spend much of his time until his death in 1971. Therese Laxalt died in 1978.

Chapter Six

Putting the City in Carson City

Carson City is flat valley to soft hills. Past the hills are the Sierra Nevada Moun-
tains. When you look up, the sky is deep blue, forever blue, and there are almost
never any clouds up there. The clouds that do come gather on top of the Sierras
and they look like wadded-up tissue paper. Every now and then, a piece of cloud
will tear away and float across the forever-blue sky.

— JENNIFER LAUCK, Blackbird: A Childhood Lost and Found

$\mathcal{T}$he last quarter of the twentieth century saw Carson City complete
the transformation from small town to small city. Between 1970
and 2000, Carson City's population increased more than threefold, from
15,468 to 52,457. Once America's smallest state capital city, Carson City
evolved into the country's twelfth smallest state capital. As its population
grew, so did the city's demand for more goods and services. National
chains flocked to the community, including major retail brand names
like Walmart, Costco, Lowe's, Home Depot, Office Depot, PetSmart, and
Target. As the community grew, it seemed to lose some of its small-town
flavor and ambience—in fact, writer Bill Bryson was so unimpressed
when he drove through in the late 1980s, that in his book *The Lost*
Continent he wrote: "Carson City was just about the most nothing little
city you could ever hope to zip through. It's the state capital, but mostly it
was just Pizza Huts and gas stations and cheap-looking casinos."

But many would argue that Bryson, who quickly passed through on
a cross-country road trip, might actually have missed out on the real
Carson City. In fact, a different view of the community appeared in the
October 2004 issue of *True West* magazine, which named the community the "best western historical site." Additionally, *The Rating Guide to*

Life in America's Small Cities, published in 1990, ranked Carson City as the nineteenth-best "micropolitan area" in the U.S. (defined by the U.S. Census Bureau as urbanized areas centered around a city or town with a population between 10,000 and 49,999) out of a total list of 219 cities. "I think history is what sets Carson City apart from other destinations in our region," according to Candace Duncan, executive director of the Carson City Convention and Visitors Bureau. "Because we've been the state capital since the 1860s and because we have so many historic buildings here from that era, it was easy for us to put that all together to promote."

The 1970s

Of course, Carson City's population and development explosion in the latter part of the twentieth century didn't happen overnight. During the decade of the 1970s, the city began to see expanded opportunities in education, cultural affairs, the arts, business, and governmental services. Carson civic leaders made their first stab at establishing a local college in 1965, when they persuaded the State Legislature to authorize the incorporation of Carson College. Unfortunately, the state provided no money for the start-up school and it folded before the completion of its first semester. The idea of an institution of higher learning in the capital city, however, proved appealing and in 1971 the University of Nevada system opened Western Nevada Community College (WNCC). The college offered a two-year program at locations in both Reno and Carson City. The latter was housed in the Civic Center and supported by a direct grant of $50,000 from the community. Additionally, the Carson City branch received a generous gift of land at the northwest part of the city.

In 1974, the Carson City classes moved into a new home, the 50,000-square-foot Bristlecone Building, on the northwest side of Eagle Valley. Two years later, the University of Nevada separated the two WNCC campuses into two units: Truckee Meadows Community College in Reno and Western Nevada Community College in Carson City. Starting in 1981, WNCC added teaching centers in Fernley, Yerington, Hawthorne, Lovelock, and Smith Valley as well as campuses in Fallon and Minden.

As the demand for training and education increased in Carson City, so did WNCC's size and scope. In 1987, Carson builders and manufacturers donated materials and labor to construct the 5,000-square-foot Woody Wurster Machine Tool Technology building, which made Western Nevada the only school in the state with such facilities and training (the school was expanded to nearly 8,500 square feet a decade later). During the 1990s, WNCC grew rapidly with the construction of additional buildings on its 160-acre campus, including the 25,000-square-foot Aspen Building (1991), the 7,652-square foot Child Development Center in 1993, the 71,000-square-foot Cedar Building (1998), the 10,000-square-foot Andi Butti Welding Technology Center in 1997, the 20,000-square-foot E. L. Cord Automotive Technology Center (1999), the Jack C. Davis Observatory (2003), and the Joe Dini Jr. Library and Student Center (2004). In 2007, the college's name was changed to Western Nevada College to reflect its expanded academic mission that included offering a new four-year Bachelor of Technology degree in construction management.

State Buildings, New and Renewed

The same year that WNCC opened, the Nevada State Legislature moved into its new home on the corner of South Carson and Fifth streets. Reno architect Graham Erskine had been hired to design the structure, which became necessary because the two branches of the state legislature had outgrown the State Capitol, where they had been meeting since 1871.

The State Legislative Building, ca. 1971. (Nevada State Archives)

The White House Hotel, a few years before it was torn down to build the State Legislative Building, 1960s. (Nevada State Archives)

Erskine, along with architects David Vhay and Raymond Hellman (who had earlier designed the Fleischmann Planetarium in Reno), created a blocky, three-story rectangular main building with two one-story, half-circle wings that housed the assembly and senate chambers.

"The building's original appearance [in 1971] was monumental and geometric," noted architectural historian Julie Nicoletta in her book *Buildings of Nevada.* "Vertical beige and brown aggregate panels, divided by bands of white stucco, covered the walls. Narrow white precast concrete panels projected beyond the windows to allow some light inside the building while lending it a fortress-like character. Designed and erected in the late 1960s when public officials in Nevada feared riots, the shielded windows and cold materials created an intended expression of aloofness."

Construction of the new Legislative Building, as well as a public plaza that eventually became a statuary park between it and the State Capitol, required demolishing the venerable White House Hotel, which had been around since 1862 but had fallen on hard times. Additionally, the state tore down a row of one- and two-story brick buildings also dating to the 1860s that once housed the offices of the *Carson Daily Appeal* and the Carson Café, a Chinese restaurant.

In 1995, legislators were again faced with a space crunch and decided to enlarge their quarters. A five-story addition was erected in front of the main rectangular part of the older building. To make the building more attractive, the concrete panels were removed and the entire building was resurfaced with pink stucco. The façade of the building was designed to complement the Capitol's appearance by incorporating a small silver-colored dome.

In addition to erecting a new Legislative Building, the state also began a $6 million reconstruction of the century-old State Capitol, which a study had concluded would not survive a modest earthquake. Beginning in 1977, the Capitol building was gutted and the roof and dome were removed. The building's stone exterior walls were reinforced with steel beams as well as rebar and concrete to withstand Mother Nature while the cupola, roof, and interior were entirely rebuilt. According to Julie Nicoletta, "Workers carefully numbered and replaced all removed pieces after installing concrete shear walls to bring the building up to modern seismic codes. Fiberglass replicas of exterior wood features, including the cupola on the capitol and the window frames, were put in place."

In 1970 the Federal Courthouse and Post Office building was turned over to the state, which converted the brick structure into a new home for the State Library in 1972. The first floor, which housed the post office, was renovated to accommodate the library's front desk as well as the periodicals room and the Nevada Room (where books about the state

Stone exterior walls of the gutted State Capitol during its overhaul, 1978. (Nevada State Archives)

were stored). The second floor, which had housed the federal courtroom and judges' chambers, became library administration offices and book storage. Other floors, long used by other federal agencies, became staff offices as well as book and periodical storage space. A large basement was also fitted to store books on movable shelves.

Community and Business Ventures

The need for a new and larger venue for community meetings and events resulted in the opening of the Carson City Community Center in January 1972. The effort to construct a multipurpose facility for meetings and conventions had begun to pick up steam in the late 1960s, when the Ormsby County Fair and Recreation Board had hired an architect to design such a building. After considerable debate about its location, the board selected a site at the northwest end of Mills Park for the $700,000 building, funded from a voter-approved bond.

The early 1970s also saw the opening of the Laxalt family's Ormsby House hotel-casino. As former senator (and governor) Paul Laxalt wrote in his memoirs, "Ormsby House had an exciting and successful start, but then the energy crisis hit. While our locals would constitute the base of our income, what would make us profitable, like all Nevada hotels, were the tourists. Since there was no air service to Carson City, we relied almost entirely on those who could reach us by car. When the gasoline crunch hit, our business, like millions of others throughout the country, was seriously hurt."

After the Laxalts sold the Ormsby to Woody Loftin in 1975, the hotel was able to turn its fortunes around by marketing itself to a more down-scale clientele. "We sold Ormsby House to an old-time Nevada gambler, Woody Loftin. He turned our elegant hotel into a 'sawdust joint,' and it became quite successful," Laxalt wrote.

Under Loftin, the Ormsby thrived for the next decade. Following his death in 1985, the property passed into the hands of his son, Truett, who embarked on an ambitious and expensive renovation program that ultimately cost him ownership of the property. By 1990, the hotel was forced into bankruptcy and it closed three years later. It reopened in 1995 under a new owner, Barry Silverton, but two years later again slipped into bankruptcy. Between 1997 and 1999, former lieutenant governor

(and later Reno mayor) Bob Cashell managed the property on behalf of
its creditors and reportedly returned it to profitability.

In 1999, Al Fiegehen and Don Lehr, owners of a Carson City–based
computer company, Cubix, purchased the hotel for $3.75 million and
announced plans to renovate it as a business-class hotel and show-
case for the community. The hotel was closed in 2000, with the owners stating that the reconstruction would be completed in about a year.
However, work continued sporadically for almost another decade. In
2003, Fiegehen and Lehr threatened to implode the building because
of their frustration with the city's building permit process. City officials
responded by agreeing to streamline the procedures.

Despite the détente, the project has yet to be completed, largely
because of unforeseen challenges in updating and rebuilding the hotel,
which was essentially gutted during the reconstruction. "It's cost a fortune for this delay," Lehr told the *Nevada Appeal* in 2008. "We just want
it finished. That's all we want."

The Kinkead Building Fiasco

By the mid-1970s, several state government agencies were again outgrowing their space, so legislators approved construction of a new state
office building on the corner of E. King and Valley streets. Named for

Nevada's third governor, John H. Kinkead, the six-story office building soon developed problems including sagging floors, a cracked and uneven foundation, falling pieces of concrete, inadequate ventilation, and leaks. Workers in the building not only complained about the building's poor air quality but also reported back problems because wheeled chairs wouldn't stay in place due to the uneven floors. By the 1990s, it was being described in news reports as the worst building ever constructed by the state. In 2005, an engineering report concluded that the Kinkead Building could collapse in a major earthquake. Additionally, state fire officials found about four hundred safety violations in the building.

In response, in 2005 state legislators agreed to relocate the 350 employees working in the building to other office space and to demolish the Kinkead. Unfortunately, while workers were moved in 2006, state budget problems prevented the building from being demolished (at an estimated cost of $1.6 million). As of late 2009, it had been "mothballed" and was still waiting to be torn down. "Working there was like being on a ship," state employee Teresa Kenedy told the Associated Press in 2006. "The building swayed. We're grateful we got out of there before it fell on our heads."

The vacant and shuttered Kinkead Building, 2009. (Richard Moreno)

The decade of the 1970s also saw the creation of a unique special event in the capital city—the Carson City International Whistle-Off, held October 1–3, 1977. Concocted by the Carson City Chamber of Commerce, the event attracted about thirty contestants its first year. According to a *Los Angeles Times* story, "Some whistled a cappella; others were accompanied by piano, guitar, banjo, washboards, taped music and even live back-up singers." The top winner during the inaugural event was an out-of-work former newspaper reporter, thirty-eight-year-old Mitch Hider of Monroe, Oregon, who performed while accompanied by a computer.

For the next decade, hundreds of whistlers flocked to Carson City to perform trilling renditions of jazz, classical, contemporary, and original compositions before crowds that numbered in the thousands. The event attracted the attention of the national news media, including *Smithsonian Magazine,* the Mike Douglas television show, *Los Angeles Times, Sacramento Bee, Minneapolis Star-Tribune, Miami Herald,* and network TV and radio programs. In the late 1980s, the event was discontinued after many contestants complained they had a difficult time performing to the best of their ability because of the dry air and high elevation.

An event of a more serious nature occurred on Wednesday, March 28, 1979, when the offices of the *Nevada Appeal* newspaper burned. The fire, which destroyed the *Appeal*'s four-year-old brick building at 200 Bath Street, started at about 11:20 PM and was believed to have been the work of an arsonist. "We know where the accelerant was put down on the floor, how he trailed it all the way down the hallway, which door it went out of and where it was lit," former Carson City Sheriff's detective Joe Curtis later told the *Appeal.* "But tying it to a person was an impossible task. There were no witnesses, nobody saw vehicles in the area."

A March 29 Associated Press story reported that "flames shot 20 to 30 feet above the roof of the Carson City *Nevada Appeal* building during the hour-long blaze." It also noted that the paper's editor, Steve Frady, was a volunteer firefighter in Virginia City, so when he learned of the fire he grabbed his helmet and gear, and "plunged into the flaming building."

The newspaper's executives and staff quickly responded to the fire by vowing to continue publishing. Immediately after the fire was extinguished, Frady dumped off his fire equipment, packed some clothing, and flew to the *Appeal*'s sister paper in Las Vegas to print the next edition, which would be flown back to Carson City for delivery on Thursday. According to later reports, "using the presses of the *Las Vegas Review-Journal,* a suite at the Frontier Motel, [city editor] Sue Morrow's home, and offices at the *Tahoe Daily Tribune,* the *Appeal* published its Thursday paper as usual with front-page photos and a story on the fire." During the following months, while its building was being reconstructed, the *Appeal* was patched together at other locations using borrowed equipment. Despite the challenges, the paper never missed an edition.

A business of an entirely different kind briefly made a splash that same year when legendary guitar maker Semie Moseley opened his Mosrite manufacturing plant in Carson City. While the factory made no lasting impression on the local economy, it did give the community a hip musical vibe for a short time. The Mosrite company was founded in California in the mid-1950s by Moseley and a partner, Rev. Ray Boatright. As a teen, Moseley had learned to repair guitars and started to build his own when he couldn't find one that felt or sounded the way he wanted. By the time he was nineteen, he had constructed his first triple-neck guitar entirely by hand. By the early 1960s, Moseley had developed the successful Mosrite Ventures model (named for a surf guitar band that first used it and made it popular), which became one of his most well-known creations.

By the early 1970s, Moseley had gone bankrupt, toured as a gospel performer, and started back up again making custom guitars. He moved his manufacturing plant to various communities during this period: to Oklahoma City in 1976, to Yuba City, California, in 1977 and, in 1979, to Carson City, Nevada. For two years, Moseley manufactured various models of Mosrite guitars in a small facility in the capital city. In 1981, the itinerant guitar man packed up and relocated once again to Jonas Ridge, North Carolina. He died in 1992 of cancer.

Perhaps the most famous single instrument Moseley ever made was produced in his Carson City shop—an electric double-neck guitar that he made for country singer Barbara Mandrell in 1981, which she is photographed playing on the back cover of her album *Barbara Mandrell Live.* The sparkling silver-and-blue instrument is on display at the National

Music Museum on the campus of the University of South Dakota in Vermillion, South Dakota.

Nevada State Railroad Museum Chugs Ahead

Some thirty years after the last Virginia & Truckee Railroad train departed from Carson City, a number of the railroad's vintage locomotives and train cars returned to the community. The occasion was the opening of the Nevada State Railroad Museum in 1980. Almost since the V&T had ceased operating and its rolling stock had been sold, railroad buffs and state historians had longed for the return of the state's most famous and historic short line. The opportunity finally came in the 1970s, when the state of Nevada was able to purchase a handful of the former V&T locomotives and cars from Paramount Pictures, which had bought them in 1938 from the railroad when it was experiencing financial problems. While owned by Paramount, the train equipment had appeared in dozens of films, including *Union Pacific* in 1939, *Meet Me in St. Louis* in 1944, *The Virginian* in 1946, and, appropriately, a western entitled *Carson City* in 1952.

After several years of promising stops and starts, the state finally funded a museum in Carson City to display the historic V&T equip-

Locomotive #8 stops near a water tower at the Nevada State Railroad Museum. (Richard Moreno)

ment. While there was some hope that the state would place the museum in the former V&T maintenance shop building at North Plaza Street, south of William Street, that plan was abandoned due to the cost of rehabilitating the shop site. Instead, the museum was located at 2180 South Carson Street, near the intersection with Stewart Street. A small group of buildings was erected to restore and interpret the equipment. In the main structure, the museum displays some of the best pieces in the collection, including the Inyo (#22), a wood-burning 1875 Baldwin 4–4–0 locomotive. This beautiful classic piece of equipment was one of five of its type purchased by the V&T in the 1870s to pull passenger cars from Reno to Virginia City. Also called the Brass Betsy, because of its elegant brass trimmings, the Inyo operated for more than fifty years before its stint in the movie industry.

In addition to the Inyo, the museum's collection includes: V&T Caboose No. 9, built in 1873; Coach No. 4, built in 1872 and one of the original sixteen passenger cars bought by the railroad; the Dayton (#18), built in 1873 and one of only two of its type still in existence; V&T Engine No. 25; V&T Flat Car #162 (built in the railroad's Carson City shops in 1891); red Caboose No. 3, from the Nevada Copper Belt Railroad, which operated in Yerington; and the Joe Douglass, a narrow-gauge locomotive built in 1882 and used on the Dayton, Sutro & Carson Valley Short Line Railroad.

The museum also has an informative exhibit describing the role of the Chinese in constructing western railroads. It includes a reconstructed Chinese joss house, which served as a community center and place of worship. In the summer months, visitors can tour the restoration shops, behind the main museum building. Inside you can view other historic rail equipment, including several boxcars and coaches (mostly non–V&T stock) awaiting restoration. Near the front of the museum building is the restored Wabuska depot, a rail worker cottage, and a reproduction of a nineteenth-century square "board and batten" water tower. During summer weekends, rides are offered on a special diesel motorcar. Additionally, on selected weekends and holidays, such as July 4th and Labor Day, the museum offers rides on the vintage equipment.

The 1980s

A celebration of the West's rich past provided Carson City with a new special event that would prove to be a major success—in fact, it commemorated its twenty-sixth anniversary in 2009. In 1983, the community established the Kit Carson Rendezvous (later known as the Carson City Rendezvous), a reenactment of a nineteenth-century mountain man encampment with participants garbed in period clothing and demonstrating various skills like panning for gold, open-fire cooking, and traditional music.

Over the years, the Rendezvous, which is held in Mills Park, has expanded to include Civil War camp and battle reenactments, Pony Express riders, Western gunfighter quick-draw competitions and demonstrations, a Native American village, a Dutch oven cook-off, stagecoach and camel rides, a western music festival, dances, an old-time fiddling contest, more than one hundred food booths, and dozens of vendors selling arts and crafts. In recent years, the Rendezvous has attracted hundreds of participants along with daily crowds of more than eight thousand.

A Native American participant smokes the peace pipe during the Kit Carson Rendezvous, ca. 1985. (Richard Moreno)

The early 1980s also saw Carson City consolidating most city departments into a complex of four office buildings on Northgate Lane. In 1982, former city manager Don Hataway recommended that the city acquire the site for $750,000, which would pay for itself in about five years because of money saved from not having to rent privately owned space for many of those city departments. At the time, Hataway said that the city would no longer need to house several departments, including his office, in the Civic Auditorium, which could be sold.

The Ormsby House and Carson Nugget gained a new rival in the early 1980s with the opening of the five-story, ninety-room Mother Lode Hotel and Casino on South Carson Street between Ninth and Tenth streets. Ormsby House owner Woody Loftin had acquired the Mother Lode a few years after it opened and operated it until his death in 1985. Two years later, the property was sold to an investment group led by Clark Russell (son of former governor Charles Russell and longtime general manager of the Ormsby House) and renamed the Carson Station. In 2002, Russell completed a major expansion of the property that included renovating the interior and exterior, enlarging the casino, and adding a restaurant. In 2006, Russell relinquished day-to-day supervision of the properties to his daughter, Jennifer Russell.

The mid-1980s also saw a group of dedicated local mothers begin an effort to develop an education-based museum for children in Carson City. The group, which originally called itself the Children's Museum of Carson (later changed to Children's Museum of Northern Nevada), conducted fundraisers and applied for state, federal, and private grants to help finance the project. Following a successful display of hands-on children-related exhibits at the Nevada State Museum, the group persuaded the city to lease the former Carson City Civic Auditorium at 813 North Carson Street to the entity for a nominal fee.

In 1988, the nonprofit museum opened with more than two dozen educational activities, including a replica of a medieval castle, working electronic and sound displays, a re-creation of a grocery store with products and a working cash register, and the Shadow Room, in which participants stand against a light-sensitive wall while a bright light flashes every couple of minutes and leaves shadows temporarily imprinted on the wall. Over the years, exhibits have been added to the museum, among them a replica of a space shuttle with a flight simulation game, a kid-size planetarium, and a large maze. Additionally, the museum offers a variety of classes and workshops.

Bullfrog County

Perhaps the most bizarre distinction ever bestowed on Carson City in the 1980s was its brief role as the county seat for a political subdivision known as Bullfrog County. In the waning hours of the 1987 legislative session, lawmakers approved the creation of a new county in Nevada, which was named Bullfrog County. The county encompassed about 144 square miles of uninhabited land in the middle of Nye County, including the proposed site of the federal government's Yucca Mountain nuclear repository. The sole purpose of the county was to allow the state to levy high taxes within its boundaries if the federal government began sending radioactive waste from nuclear reactors around the country to Yucca Mountain. State lawmakers concocted the scheme in response to overtures that some Nye County officials had made to the U.S. government that they would accept the Yucca Mountain project in return for generous federal payments. According to news reports, this money would have gone directly to Nye County and not to the state, which opposed the dump.

"When legislators formed this new county out of the bleak and hostile desert north of Las Vegas in June, they did not worry about soliciting the views of local residents. There are no residents," noted Thomas J. Knudson in an August 30, 1987, article in the *New York Times*. "There are also no roads, no buildings, no sign of life whatever except for a few jack rabbits, rattlesnakes and lizards. But there is one heck of a tax rate. That was the point when the Legislature created Bullfrog County two months ago; to set up a jurisdiction with property taxes so high that the Federal Government wouldn't want to pay the price—up to $25 million a year, theoretically.

Legislators involved Carson City in the plan when they placed the county seat in the capital city, located about 270 miles northwest of Bullfrog, and gave the authority to appoint county commissioners to the governor. Governor Richard Bryan, who signed the legislation into law, appointed a three-member county commission. Nye County officials, however, immediately filed a lawsuit challenging the creation of Bullfrog County on thirty-seven different legal grounds, including the argument that the appointment of the county commission violated the constitutional right to representative government. On February 11, 1988, Judge David Zenoff sided with Nye County, ruling the law was unconstitutional. "I cannot in good conscience uphold this law," Judge Zenoff said. "There's too much hanging in mid-air. There's nothing definite and concrete."

Following the decision, Governor Bryan issued a statement saying, "This apparently resolves the Bullfrog County issue unless the Legislature chooses to appeal." Legislators, however, quietly voted to repeal the legislation during their next biennial session in 1989. With that action, one might say that Bullfrog County had finally croaked.

THE END OF THE DECADE coincided with the commemoration of the State of Nevada's 125th anniversary in 1989. Carson City artist Verne Horton designed the official logo for the celebration, which was used on state highway welcome signs and a wide variety of publications and products. The celebration, spearheaded by Secretary of State Frankie Sue Del Papa, produced special commemorative items: historic videos, firearms, and posters, as well as a full-color commemorative license plate— the first produced by the state. A special 125th Anniversary Committee, appointed by the governor, distributed proceeds from the sales of the plates, which were sold for only one year (October 31, 1989, to October 31, 1990), to projects and organizations that advanced the state's history or culture.

The 1990s

Perhaps no action generated as much controversy in Carson City as the destruction of the historic Virginia & Truckee Railroad maintenance shops in 1990. Largely abandoned since 1950, the iconic stone structure—often referred to as the V&T's roundhouse, despite its rectangular shape—was in poor condition. The owners, Mrs. Omer Wolf and Paul Larquier (children of Paul Louis Larquier, who had purchased the site in 1955), had sought to develop the property but several proposals fell through.

"Public acquisition was attempted at least once, with the idea of a V&T museum in mind, but the effort failed due to the owner's high price demands," wrote Bob Yarger, editor of the *Railway Preservation News,* an online magazine of railroad history. "One of the last efforts was a private venture to turn it into a casino/shopping facility, with a V&T locomotive on display inside. That too never happened, and the structure fell into further disrepair. One section of the roof fell in, there was a fire, and the city declared it an unsafe structure. In the end, the heirs of the original owner had it taken down in exchange for the stone blocks, which were reportedly sold to wineries in the Napa Valley. Thus, the magnificent, historic structure, built of sandstone blocks hand-quarried by prison labor, was no more.

In response to the loss of the V&T shops and other historic struc-tures in Carson City, the decade of the 1990s brought a new appreciation for the community's rich past. In 1989, the Loma Prieta earthquake in northern California damaged the 120-year-old former Carson City Mint building, which housed the Nevada State Museum. The *Nevada Appeal* reported that the earthquake "caused structural damage that threatened to separate floors and the roof from the sandstone walls." In response, the state hired a Reno contractor in 1992 to install hundreds of steel braces and straps that stabilized the building by interconnecting the walls, floors, and roof. During the reconstruction, all of the museum's exhibits were taken apart and removed. The museum, however, was able to reopen about a year later.

The V&T Reborn

The Virginia & Truckee Railroad proved to be a real-life example of the little engine that could. In the 1970s, California businessman and rail-road fan Robert Gray began slowly reconstructing the historic railroad. He purchased the old right-of-ways, laid new tracks, and purchased a vintage steam locomotive, which became part of a revived V&T tour-ist excursion railroad between Virginia City and Gold Hill. He laid the first tie in 1974 and started running his train for tourists three years later. Over the next two decades, he slowly expanded the line so that passen-gers could travel from a small depot in Virginia City on F Street, south of the St. Mary's in the Mountain Catholic Church, to the Gold Hill Depot, a thirty-five-minute trip that covered about six miles.

In the early 1990s, V&T enthusiasts, along with Storey County, Carson City, and state officials, began studying the possibility of rebuild-ing the historic rail line between Virginia City and Carson City. In 2001, the nonprofit Nevada Commission for the Reconstruction of the V&T Railway was created to raise money and oversee the project, which will have cost $60–$70 million when completed in about 2012. From 2001 to 2005, the railroad made slow progress as the commission acquired right-of-way easements and financial commitments. In 2005, the Nevada

Department of Transportation awarded a $3.8 million contract to extend the railroad south from Gold Hill. The contract included filling in a huge open-pit mine called the Overman Pit, which had blocked previous efforts to lengthen the railroad (the pit had been dug after the railroad was abandoned). Additionally, the commission purchased a 1914 Baldwin steam locomotive from a defunct northern California tourist railroad.

In the middle of the decade, the Nevada Legislature provided $500,000 in additional funds to help keep the project going while the Department of Transportation donated a railroad bridge (formerly located in southern Nevada) to be used for a crossing over U.S. 50. The legislature also granted Carson City permission to raise its sales tax by one-eighth of a cent to fund a big portion of the remaining expenses. According to the *Reno Gazette-Journal,* the project was funded from a variety of sources including state and federal transportation money and sales tax revenue from both Carson City and Storey County.

The reconstructed railroad began running trains between Virginia City and Carson City on August 14, 2009. The route incorporates the Virginia & Truckee Railroad's 2.5 miles of existing track from Virginia City to the Gold Hill Depot and then crosses the filled-in Overman Pit. From there, it continues through American Flat, a former mining mill district near Silver City, before reaching U.S. 50 near Mound House.

The V&T Railway bridge spanning U.S. 50 in east Carson City. (Richard Moreno)

At that point the route crosses the highway on the refurbished railroad bridge and takes riders on a temporary track to the Eastgate Siding Depot on Flint Drive located at the far eastern edge of Carson City. According to Dwight Millard, chairman of the Nevada Commission for Reconstruction of the V&T Railway, the final track will go to a depot site farther west in Carson City near Drako Way. This final phase of the project is expected to be completed by 2012.

The Kit Carson Trail

The city's decision to preserve and promote its history was also reflected in the Carson City Convention and Visitors Bureau's creation of the Kit Carson Trail, an interpretive 2.5-mile walking tour of the city's most historic neighborhoods. In the early 1990s, the bureau painted a thick blue line on the sidewalks of the city's most historic neighborhoods. About five dozen homes and buildings are marked on a free full-color, illustrated tour map distributed by the bureau. Additionally, the bureau provides a "Talking Houses" podcast of sixteen segments describing the most interesting historic structures along the route. Motorists can also tune their car radios to a frequency (AM 1020, AM 1040, AM 1060, or AM 1080) to listen to the informative ninety-second narratives.

"Nevada's capital takes history pretty seriously—if for no other reason than because Reno and Las Vegas have little of it and even less aptitude for storing and exhibiting it," noted *San Francisco Chronicle* writer Spud Hilton in 2006. "The Blue Line Trail, a self-guided circuit around the Historic District that passes dozens of pre-1900 homes is an easy morning's walk. My wife, Ann, and I picked up the trail outside the Bliss Mansion and sauntered down shady streets dusted with rustling fall leaves, past more picket fences than in 'Leave it to Beaver.'"

In 1993, the bureau developed regular, guided, ninety-minute "Ghost Walk" tours of the historic district (usually offered each year in late May and near Nevada Day in October). The guides, mostly local professional actors, are dressed in period clothing and "channel" the spirits of long-dead prominent Carsonites. Along the way, other "ghosts" appear in the various historic venues and share their stories of the past.

Not all of Carson City's development activity during the decade centered on history. In 1991, a new Supreme Court Building was erected on the site of the Nye Building. The four-story structure, designed by the local architecture firm of Eissmann-Pence, serves as the eastern side of the Capitol Complex, with the State Capitol and the State Library and Archives to the north and the State Legislative Building to the south. While the building provided much-needed additional space to the Supreme Court and its staff, its design didn't impress some traditionalists. "Like the recently renovated State Legislative Building (late 1990s) and the State Library (1993) next door, the Supreme Court displays a late twentieth-century tendency toward the banal in public buildings in the Capitol Complex," wrote architectural historian Julie Nicoletta. "Limited budgets and the desire on the part of architects and legislators to erect buildings that will not offend have produced results unworthy of the earlier tradition of small but elegantly designed structures."

The 120,000-square-foot Supreme Court has a basement parking garage, a large law library on the first floor, a two-story courtroom on the second floor, and justices' chambers and legal staff offices on the third

The new Supreme
Court Building, 2008.
(Richard Moreno)

floor. At the center of the building is a three-story rotunda paved with colored granite. Inset into the marble floor of this public area is a 1,700-pound bronze relief of the state seal. The exterior of the building features a prominent portico entrance with four bays on each side, which are defined by large, unadorned piers.

At nearly the same time as the new Supreme Court was under construction, the state began building a new Nevada State Library and Archives directly east of the State Capitol to house the state's collection of books, federal and state government publications, and state archives. The new 130,000-square-foot building was needed because the department had outgrown its quarters in the former Federal Building. The $15.2 million structure incorporated the historic former State Printing Office, which had been built in 1885–86 and had previously housed the state archives. It allowed the library to consolidate with the Nevada State Archives and be adjacent to the Nevada State Historic Preservation Office in the old state printing building.

In 1992, the city opened the covered and partially enclosed Pony Express Pavilion at the east edge of Mills Park. Despite considerable controversy, Mayor Marv Teixeira spearheaded the effort to build the 31,020-square-foot multipurpose facility, which has hosted concerts, a regular farmers' market, political rallies (vice presidential candidate Sarah Palin appeared there in 2008), an in-line hockey league, and a number of special events including the Carson City Library's annual Oktoberfest celebration and the Silver Dollar Car Classic auto show.

That same year, the city also approved construction of a new Carson City Public Safety Complex to replace an aging facility constructed in 1966. The original law enforcement building at East Musser and Roop streets had been built to accommodate consolidation of the Ormsby County Sheriff and Carson City Police operations and expanded in the early 1980s. By the end of the decade, however, it had become obvious that the community needed a larger and more modern jail and more law enforcement offices. Built in phases, the facility, which incorporated the First Judicial District Court, Justice Court, and Municipal Court, was completed in March 1999.

After years of discussion and debate, the city moved forward in the mid-1990s with plans to create a new City Hall using an abandoned Bank of America building on the corner of Carson and East Musser streets, across from the Nevada State Capitol. Starting a few years earlier, city officials had attempted to establish a City Hall closer to downtown—even trying to persuade the state to sell it the Old Federal Building—because some believed the Northgate Lane city offices were too far removed from the town center. In 1996, the city bought the bank for $1.25 million and spent an additional $607,000 remodeling the structure. As part of the work, the bank building was retrofitted with a "turn-of-the-century" look incorporating a red-brick façade and window arches designed to echo the former V&T Railroad roundhouse that had been torn down a few years earlier. "It fits very much the look of the new downtown," City Manager John Berkich told the *Nevada Appeal*.

The opening of Piñon Plaza in 1995 was the first new casino project in Carson City in more than a decade. Located on U.S. 50, east of the city center, Piñon Plaza was also the first major resort development built specifically to take advantage of the construction of the long-proposed U.S. 395 bypass, which diverted traffic from Carson Street through the middle of the city to a new elevated highway on the east side of the community. When it opened, Piñon Plaza, originally owned by Clark Russell, offered a casino, a thirty-two-lane bowling alley, and a seventy-space recreational vehicle park. It quickly expanded, adding restaurants and a sixty-five-room hotel in 1998, which was expanded by another eighty-four rooms a year later. In 2006, Russell sold Piñon Plaza to Jacobs Entertainment, a national gaming company, and the property was renamed Gold Dust West.

The end of the decade saw the revitalization of a landmark building in Carson City that had been vacant for several years. The former U.S. Courthouse and Post Office at 401 N. Carson Street, which was completed in 1891 and had been used as the State Library since 1972, sat empty for nearly five years while the state decided what to do with it. In 1997, the Nevada Commission on Tourism embarked on a $1.5 million project to restore and rehabilitate the structure for its offices. The work included renovating the former courtroom on the second floor into a formal commission meeting room. When the building reopened in 1999, it was renamed in honor of former senator (and governor) Paul Laxalt, who grew up in Carson City and had practiced law in the courtroom.

Today, the four-story brick building is home to the Commission on Tourism staff as well as the state-owned *Nevada Magazine.*

The 2000s

The new millennium ushered in a wave of changes to the capital city. Reflecting shifts in the city's growth patterns—much of the new development was to the south and east—the city saw the opening of a substantial number of new retail and commercial businesses, including the arrival of many regional and national chain stores, as well as several new casinos. The impetus for this new growth was the increasing population at the north end of Douglas County (in the Indian Hills area, directly south of the southernmost Carson City limit) and in the town of Dayton in Lyon County (directly east). Additionally, the construction of the first phase of the U.S. 395 bypass, which was completed in 2006, spurred development to the east at the intersection of U.S. 395 and U.S. 50.

Also reflecting the changing nature of the capital city, the venerable St. Teresa of Avila Catholic Church relocated from its historic quarters in the center of the city at 400 West King Street to a larger church building at 3000 N. Lompa Lane, east of town, in 2002. The move was necessitated by the congregation's need for more space. The new facility, which cost $5.5 million, included a one-thousand-seat church, office space, and a social hall. The historic church building, erected in 1872 and enlarged over the years, was sold to the nonprofit Brewery Arts Center, which, in 2004, converted it into a four-hundred-seat performing arts hall. In 2008, the BAC gained conditional approval from the city for a $3.5 million expansion that includes a four-hundred-seat outdoor amphitheater between the Brewery Arts Center main building (the old Carson Brewery) and the performance hall. The project would involve permanently closing South Minnesota Street between Second and King streets.

The most significant of Carson's most recent casino developments was the opening in 2003 of the Fandango Casino inside a former Supply One hardware store near the south end of the city. Initially developed in two phases, the Fandango opened with a modest 10,000-square-foot casino and two restaurants but expanded within a few months to include another 21,000 square feet of cabaret, bar, and dance floor space as well as a 340-seat buffet. Within another couple of months, the property, owned by Carson Gaming, a Las Vegas investment group, had added a steak house and a larger race and sports book, and the establishment had grown to more than 60,000 square feet. Within four years of its opening, Fandango had added a $4 million three-story parking garage as well as a $14 million ten-screen multiplex movie theater, yet another expansion of the casino (an additional 13,000 square feet) and an $11 million one-hundred-room Courtyard by Marriott hotel.

It was a hotel-casino project that was never built that generated the most heat in 2003. That summer, Max Baer Jr., a former producer and television star (he played "Jethro Bodine" in *The Beverly Hillbillies*) and son of a former heavyweight champion of the world, announced he and his partners had purchased a vacant Walmart building in the Southgate Shopping Center on the south end of Carson City and wanted to replace it with a $54 million *Beverly Hillbillies*–themed hotel-casino. Baer's plans included a 30,000-square-foot casino, a 240-room hotel, restaurants, lounges, nightclub, wedding chapel, arcade, and multiscreen movie theater. A few years earlier, Baer had proposed a similar project for an aging shopping mall site in Reno, but it had failed due to a lack of funding and the city's resistance to some of his design ideas, such as a flaming two-hundred-foot oil derrick.

Baer's Carson City proposal was equally snakebitten. After purchasing the Walmart site, he encountered opposition from the other Southgate tenants, which included a J.C. Penney's store, because the proposal violated the mall's building restrictions, which specifically prohibited nightclubs, theaters, casinos, or other similar operations. In 2004, a Carson City judge sided with the other tenants and ruled that the project would violate the shopping center rules. Despite the ruling, Baer continued to insist for a few more years that he would build his hotel-casino, but he finally sold the site in 2007 (it reopened as a Burlington Coat Factory in 2008). He shifted his attention to Douglas County, acquiring a site east of U.S. 395 between Topsy Lane and North Sunridge Drive.

In 2007, Douglas County approved a new Beverly Hillbillies proposal, which included a 270,000-square-foot hotel-casino. The project, however, was held up by a lawsuit filed by an adjacent housing development company that argued the massive resort was incompatible with the single-family homes it planned to construct. In 2008, the county resolved the dispute by changing the zoning on the development company's property to allow mixed-use commercial and multifamily dwellings, which would be more compatible with the hotel-casino project. As of 2009, work had not begun on Jethro's Beverly Hillbillies Mansion and Casino due to tightening credit markets as a result of a national economic recession. Baer, however, insisted that the project would still be built.

In 2005, the State of Nevada once again recognized the need for more office space for state employees and erected the Richard H. Bryan Building at 902 S. Stewart Street, adjacent to the Nevada Department of Transportation complex. The 120,000-square-foot building, which houses the Conservation and Natural Resources Department divisions, including Environmental Protection, Water Resources, and State Parks, was financed via a lease-purchase agreement. Under the terms of the arrangement, one of the first for the state, the five-story structure, which cost $20 million, will be paid for by the state over twenty-seven years. With interest the total price tag will be about $44 million.

Late that same year, Carson City gained a state-of-the-art medical facility with the opening of the $118 million Carson Tahoe Regional Medical Center at the north edge of the community, just off the newly completed bypass. The 352,000-square-foot, eighty-five-acre hospital complex opened with 144 beds (138 private rooms) as well as a larger emergency room, new cardiology facility, cancer center, surgical center, and more-comprehensive imaging services. Within a year of the hospital's opening, a 40,000-square-foot medical office building was erected on the west side of the surgery center. In 2006–07, the Merriner family donated more than $2 million to construct fourteen cottages on the hospital campus to house people from outside the community who must travel to the medical center for cancer treatments.

The last major gaming development of the decade was the construction of the $20 million, 30,000-square-foot Bodine's Casino on the corner of South Carson Street and Clear Creek Road in south Carson City in 2008. In addition to the casino, the project included a Chicago-style pub with a pizzeria, two bars, and a sports and race book. The three-acre site, adjacent to Fuji Park, was long the home to a popular local restaurant and bar by the same name. Ironically, when the project was announced, both Max Baer Jr., developer of the proposed Beverly Hillbillies Mansion and Casino, and the CBS Corporation, which owns the rights to the original *Beverly Hillbillies* program and its characters (including Jethro Bodine, the character played by Baer), threatened to sue the owners unless they changed the name. Bodine's co-owners Mike Pegram and the Carano family (owners of the Eldorado Hotel Casino and Silver Legacy Resort in Reno) dismissed the claim, citing the fact that the earlier Bodine's bar and restaurant had been around since 1985 and the property was named after one of the original owners and not the 1960s television program.

The Carson City Bypass

Beginning in the late 1950s, Carson City community leaders discussed the notion of a parkway or bypass around the downtown. At the time, Carson City was still a small town of less than five thousand residents but forward-thinking planners saw a day when narrow, two-lane Carson Street—the main artery between Reno and Douglas County—would become a traffic bottleneck. Former state archivist Guy Rocha has written about a planning study published in 1958 that offered the first written suggestion of a ring road to the east of the city's core. He said a proposed county master development plan in 1964 indicated an "Eagle

Valley freeway" but the idea was shot down by downtown business interests that felt it was premature to try to divert traffic from the city center. The concept was revived in the 1980s, once the city's population had surpassed thirty thousand residents and the downtown streets were starting to show signs of congestion.

In 1997, Carson City residents took a huge step toward making the bypass a reality when they agreed to a local gas tax increase to pay for a portion of building the road, which had an estimated total cost of about $330 million. Intense lobbying by city officials led to state transportation officials agreeing to give the bypass a high priority. Using a combination of state, federal, and local dollars, the Nevada Department of Transportation completed planning work and erected several bridges along the route by 2002. A year later, the department began work on the first phase of the four-lane Carson City Freeway (its formal name), which included building a 4.6-mile stretch of freeway from Lakeview to U.S. 50. Following the completion of that phase in 2006, the department began work on Phase 2A of the bypass, which included completion of an interchange at U.S. 50 and extension of the freeway to Fairview Drive. This part of the project opened on September 24, 2009. The final part of the project, Phase 2B, will include completion of the freeway from Fairview Drive to South Carson Street. The department anticipates the project being completed by 2014, depending on the availability of funding.

IN 2008, Carson City celebrated its sesquicentennial. The little trading post in an eastern Sierra valley that had been named after a dead bird, birthed by a transplanted New Yorker turned land speculator, and given substance by the overachieving family of a Basque sheepherder, had thrived for a century and a half. Unlike many neighboring northern Nevada communities that had blossomed at the same time—only to die or slowly fade away—Carson City had not only survived, it had prospered.

And it was still a mighty polite town.

Selected Bibliography

Books

A Complete Official Road Guide of the Lincoln Highway. 5th ed., 1924. Reprint,
Tooele, Utah: Patrice Press, 1993.

Angel, Myron, ed. *Thompson & West's History of Nevada.* 1881. Reprint, Berkeley:
Howell-North, 1958.

Ansari, Mary B. *Carson City Place Names: The Names of Old Ormsby County,
Nevada.* Reno: Camp Nevada, 1995.

Browne, J. Ross. *A Peep at Washoe: Sketches of Virginia City, Nevada Territory.*
1860. Las Vegas: Nevada Publications, 1986.

———. *Washoe Revisited.* 1864.
http://www.archive.org/details/washoerevisitedoobrowrich
(accessed May 10, 2009).

Bryson, Bill. *The Lost Continent: Travels in Small Town America.* New York:
Harper Perennial, 1989.

Carlson, Helen. *Nevada Place Names.* Reno: University of Nevada Press, 1974.

Cerveri, Doris. *With Curry's Compliments: The Story of Abraham Curry.* Elko,
Nev.: Nostalgia Press, 1990.

Curran, Jack. *Back to the Twenties: His Memories of Growing Up in Carson City.*
Virginia City, Nev.: Above and Beyond, 1994.

Davis, Sam P., ed. *History of Nevada.* 2 vols. 1913. Reprint, Las Vegas: Nevada
Publications, 1984.

Dirlik, Arif, ed., assisted by Malcolm Yeung. *Chinese on the American Frontier.*
Lanham, Md.: Rowman & Littlefield, 2001.

Drury, Wells. *An Editor on the Comstock Lode.* New York: Farrar & Rinehart,
1936.

Egan, Ferol. *Sand in a Whirlwind: The Paiute Indian War of 1860.* 1972. Reprinted
with foreword by Sessions Wheeler. Reno: University of Nevada Press,
1985.

Elliott, Russell. *History of Nevada.* Lincoln: University of Nebraska Press, 1987.

Goodwin, Charles Carroll. *As I Remember Them.* Salt Lake City: Originally published by a Special Committee of the Salt Lake Commercial Club, 1913. www.nevadaobserver.com/Reading%20Room%20Documents/as_i_remember_them_toc.htm (accessed May 10, 2009).

Heller, Dean. *Political History of Nevada, 1996.* 10th ed. Issued by the Nevada Secretary of State. Carson City: State Printing Office, 1997.

Hickson, Howard. *Mint Mark: "CC": The Story of the United States Mint at Carson City, Nevada.* Edited by Guy Shipler. Carson City: Nevada State Museum, 1972.

Highton, Jake. *Nevada Newspaper Days: A History of Journalism in the Silver State.* Stockton, Calif.: Heritage West Books, 1990.

Hulse, James W. *Oases of Culture: A History of Public and Academic Libraries in Nevada.* Reno: University of Nevada Press, 2003.

———. *The Silver State: Nevada's Heritage Reinterpreted.* 2d ed. Reno: University of Nevada Press, 1998.

Hulse, James, with Leonard E. Goodall and Jackie Allen. *Reinventing the System: Higher Education in Nevada, 1968–2000.* Reno: University of Nevada Press, 2002.

James, Ronald M. *The Roar and the Silence: A History of Virginia City and the Comstock Lode.* Reno: University of Nevada Press, 1998.

———. *Temples of Justice: County Courthouses of Nevada.* University of Nevada Press, 1994.

Kelly, J. Wells. *First Directory of Nevada Territory.* 1862. Reprint, Los Gatos, Calif.: Talisman Press, 1962.

Lauck, Jennifer. *Blackbird: A Childhood Lost and Found.* New York: Washington Square Press, 2001.

Laxalt, Paul. *Nevada's Paul Laxalt: A Memoir.* Reno: Jack Bacon & Company, 2000.

Laxalt, Robert. *The Basque Hotel.* Reno: University of Nevada Press, 1989.

———. *The Governor's Mansion.* Reno: University of Nevada Press, 1994.

———. *Sweet Promised Land.* New York: Harper & Row, 1957.

———. *Travels with My Royal: A Memoir of the Writing Life.* Reno: University of Nevada Press, 2001.

Lingenfelter, Richard E., and Karen Rix Gash. *The Newspapers of Nevada: A History & Bibliography 1854–1979.* Reno: University of Nevada Press, 1984.

Lord, Eliot. *Comstock Mining and Miners: The Comprehensive History of Virginia City's Mining Industry.* 1883. Reprint, Berkeley: Howell-North, 1959.

Marschall, John P. *Jews in Nevada: A History.* Reno: University of Nevada Press, 2008.

Mathews, Mary McNair. *Ten Years in Nevada: or, Life on the Pacific Coast.* 1880. Reprint, Lincoln: University of Nebraska Press, 1985.

Moe, Albert Woods. *Nevada's Golden Age of Gambling.* Angel Fire, N.M.: Puget Sound Books, 2001.

Myrick, David F. *Railroads of Nevada and Eastern California.* Vol. 1, *The Northern Roads.* Berkeley: Howell-North, 1962.

Nicoletta, Julie. *Buildings of Nevada.* Photographs by Bret Morgan. New York: Oxford University Press, 2000.

Oldham, Willa. *Carson City: Nevada's Capital City.* Carson City: Nevada State Museum, 1992.

———. *Carson Tahoe Hospital: The Story of a Caring Community.* Edited by Philip M. Lehrman. Genoa, Nev.: Desk Top Publishers, 1987.

Paine, Albert Bigelow. 1912. *Mark Twain, A Biography: The Personal and Literary Life of Samuel Langhorne Clemens.* New York: Harper, 1912. http://www.gutenberg.org/etext/2988 (accessed July 2009).

Rice, Harvey. *Letters from the Pacific Slope, or First Impressions.* New York: D. Appleton & Co., 1870.

Stewart, William M. *Reminiscences of Senator William M. Stewart, of Nevada.* Edited by George Rothwell Brown. New York: Neale Publishing Company, 1908.

Twain, Mark. *Roughing It.* 1872. Foreword by Leonard Kriegel. New York: New American Library, 1962.

Wade, Edwin L., and Carol Haralson, eds. *The Arts of the North American Indian: Native Traditions in Evolution.* Manchester, Vt.: Hudson Hills Press, 1986.

Waldorf, John Taylor. *A Kid on the Comstock: Reminiscences of a Virginia City Childhood.* Palo Alto, Calif.: American West Publishing Company, 1970.

Wright, William [Dan De Quille, pseud.]. *History of the Big Bonanza.* 1876. Reprint, New York: A. A. Knopf, 1947.

Wurm, Ted, and Harre W. Demoro. *The Silver Short Line: A History of the Virginia & Truckee Railroad.* 1983. Reprint, Virginia City, Nev.: Virginia & Truckee Railroad, 1988.

Yarger, Bob. "Back to California—Part 3 of 3." *Railway Preservation News: Online magazine of railway history and preservation* (posted December 1, 2003). http://www.rypn.org/ (accessed June 4, 2009).

Zanjani, Sally. *Devils Will Reign: How Nevada Began.* Reno: University of Nevada Press, 2006.

Periodicals

Adler, Lee. "3,000 tour hospital during open house." *Nevada Appeal,* November 11, 1968.

———. "City-County Join." *Nevada Appeal,* July 1, 1969.

Baker, Dennis. "Old Carson High School building posing problems for neighborhood." *Nevada Appeal,* March 24, 1971.

Ballew, Sue. "A visit to King's Canyon and its rich history." *Nevada Appeal,* November 9, 2008.

Bayer, Chris. "Major Ormsby's dream." *Nevada Appeal,* May 18, 2008, and May 25, 2008.

Bosshart, Becky. "Carano family partners in Bodine's casino." *Nevada Appeal,* March 13, 2007.

———. "Fandango breaks ground on $11 M hotel." *Nevada Appeal,* December 29, 2006.

———. "Lompa Ranch history goes back to 1936." *Nevada Appeal,* September 2, 2006.

———. "Lompa Ranch on the market for development." *Nevada Appeal,* September 2, 2006.

———. "Passing the business to the next generation." *Nevada Appeal,* January 5, 2006.

———. "The top 10 business stories of 2005." *Nevada Appeal,* January 1, 2006.

Bovee, Rex. "Plans announced for new home for St. Teresa's." *Nevada Appeal,* October 7, 1999.

"Bypass reshapes Carson's business landscapes." *Nevada Appeal,* November 17, 2005.

"California firm is low bidder on new high school." *Nevada Appeal,* February 8, 1956.

"Carson business 'terrific,' says Nugget owner." *Nevada Appeal,* August 4, 1954.

"Carson City is growing." *Nevada Appeal,* February 16, 1956.

"Carson Mall opening set." *Nevada Appeal,* March 23, 1966.

"Carson-Tahoe Hospital and Carson Tahoe Regional Medical Center timeline." *Nevada Appeal,* December 4, 2005.

"Center center gets another $1 million." *Las Vegas Review-Journal,* December 29, 2005.

"Chamber endorses local college." *Nevada Appeal,* March 10, 1966.

"Civic Center hearing: Pros outnumber cons." *Nevada Appeal,* October 29, 1968.

"Consolidation gets big statewide endorsement." *Nevada Appeal,* November 6, 1968.

"Convention center gets nod; advertising promotion eyed." *Nevada Appeal,* March 15, 1966.

Costa-Landers, Rhonda. "The end of an era for St. Teresa of Avila." *Nevada Appeal,* March 7, 2007.

Curry, John Penn. *Gazlay's Pacific Monthly.* January–June 1865.

Dornan, Geoff. "Longtime rancher 'Dutch' Borda dies." *Nevada Appeal,* December 28, 2004.

Earl, Phillip I. "Nevada's 'other' opera house boasts colorful past." *Reno Gazette-Journal,* March 13, 1988.

Egbert, Barbara. "Purchase of offices by city touted as big money saver." *Nevada Appeal,* July 9, 1982.

"Foes, backers clash at consolidation meeting." *Nevada Appeal,* October 27, 1968.

"Footprints of Monster Men." *New York Times,* August 18, 1882.

Fox, Kara. "Legendary basket weaver's art displayed." *Tahoe Bonanza,* April 29, 2004.

Frank, Dave. "At least I got them 52 acres of park." *Nevada Appeal,* April 19, 2008.

———. "Bodine's casino opens." *Nevada Appeal,* May 8, 2008.

———. "Bodine's to CBS: Name not changing." *Nevada Appeal,* August 21, 2007.

———. "Brewery Arts Center moves forward with expansion." *Nevada Appeal,* November 20, 2008.

———. "Brewery Arts Center wants to build 400-seat amphitheater." *Nevada Appeal,* October 11, 2008.

———. "It had nothing to do with 'The Beverly Hillbillies.'" *Nevada Appeal,* August 22, 2007.

———. "Nugget has long history in Carson City." *Nevada Appeal,* November 16, 2008.

"Good Place to Live." *Nevada Appeal,* January 2, 1951.

"Groundbreaking today launches new DMV headquarters building." *Nevada Appeal,* June 28, 1965.

Hammon, Amanda. "Plaza hotel casino expansion breaks ground." *Nevada Appeal,* November 9, 1999.

"Highway Department into new building May 10." *Nevada Appeal,* May 7, 1965.

"Hillbillies Casino on the ropes, but not out." *Nevada Appeal,* May 6, 2009.

Hilton, Spud. "Nevada history still kicking in Carson City: Comstock era comes to life on Blue Line Trail." *San Francisco Chronicle,* November 19, 2006.

Keller, Jill. "Carson City ranch must make way for freeway bypass." *Associated Press,* December 29, 2002.

Knudson, Thomas J. "Bullfrog County, Nev., (Pop. 0) Fights Growth." *New York Times,* August 30, 1987.

Lufrano, Jill. "Judge: Baer casino violates shopping center rules." *Nevada Appeal,* August 3, 2004.

"Nevada County is held illegal." *Associated Press,* February 13, 1988.

"New owners will add to the Pinon Plaza, manager says." *Nevada Appeal,* February 14, 2006.

"Old Wal-Mart sold for $8.5 M." *Nevada Appeal,* May 16, 2007.

Richards, Bob. "Carson City: Nevada's lovely little capital." *The Nevadan,* July 21, 1963.

Rosenthal, Brian. "V&T railroad to resume Carson-Virginia City route after 71 years." *Reno Gazette-Journal,* July 29, 2009.

Smith, Bob. "New state office building under fire by planning board and legislators." *Nevada Appeal,* February 17, 1956.

"Spacious, new office structure has 120 rooms of various size, shape." *Nevada Appeal,* July 6, 1951.

"State building named in honor of Richard Bryan." *Las Vegas Sun,* July 15, 2005.

Steele, Patti. "Carson tries auction to shed old city hall." *Reno Gazette-Journal,* May 2, 1997.

———. "City Hall overhaul on target." *Reno Gazette-Journal,* April 18, 1997.

Tillotson, Ron. "Just a Winnemucca Cowboy." *Nevada Magazine,* March–April 1981.

Toll, David W. "E. E. Roberts and the Politics of Personal Liberty." *Nevada Magazine,* November–December 1982.

"Twain Would Ride with Monk's Ghost." *Washington Times,* September 17, 1903.

Vasquez, Susie. "Baer makes his case before Rotary Club." *Nevada Appeal,* December 31, 2003.

———. "Casino Fandango to open in old Supply One." *Nevada Appeal,* June 3, 2006.

———. "Fandango Phase II nears completion; casino proves big hit." *Nevada Appeal,* November 24, 2003.

———. "Music to ring through St. Teresa hall once more." *Nevada Appeal,* January 24, 2002.

———. "Plans for Beverly Hillbillies Mansion & Casino revealed." *Nevada Appeal,* August 16, 2003.

Vogel, Ed. "Remembering a basket weaver's magic." *Las Vegas Review-Journal,* August 27, 2001.

"Vote Yes on Proposition Three." *Nevada Appeal,* October 29, 1968.

Westergard, Tammy. "Suit Up: Carson High Senators pick up the political game." *Carson Magazine,* Spring 2005.

Electronic Material

Allen, Richard. Richard "Tennessee" Allen Papers, 1857–1860. http://www
.nevadaobserver.com/Reading%20Room%20Documents/The%20
Tennessee%20Letters%20%281983%29%20Part%2001.html (accessed May
10, 2009).

Bell, Dennis. "The Man Who Invented the Wheel and Paid the Price." http://
freepages.genealogy.rootsweb.ancestry.com/~wanda/ferriswheel.html
(accessed June 24, 2009).

Hawley, Tom. "Bullfrog County." News Channel 3 (Las Vegas), August 28, 2008.
www.kvbc.com (accessed June 24, 2009).

Nevada Women's History Project. Online biographies of Hannah Clapp, Dat
So La Lee, Nellie Mighels Davis, Therese Alpetche Laxalt, Jennie O'Hare
Riordan, and Marjorie Ann Russell. www.unr.edu/nwhp/biographies/htm
(accessed June 3, 2009).

Rocha, Guy Louis. Myth #13, "George W. G. Ferris, Jr. and the Ferris Wheel."
Nevada State Library and Archives, Historical Myth a Month. www
.nevadaculture.org (accessed June 20, 2009).

———. Myth #18, "Is There Anything Traditional about Nevada Day?"
Nevada State Library and Archives, Historical Myth a Month. www
.nevadaculture.org (accessed December 22, 2009).

———. Myth #24, "Eagle Valley and Carson City." Nevada State Library and
Archives, Historical Myth a Month. www.nevadaculture.org (accessed
December 22, 2009).

———. Myth #28, "Las Vegas: Nevada's Next State Capital?" Nevada State Library
and Archives, Historical Myth a Month. www.nevadaculture.org (accessed
July 6, 2009).

———. Myth #31, "Nevada's 'Silver' Capital 'Dome.'" Nevada State Library and
Archives, Historical Myth a Month. www.nevadaculture.org (accessed
December 22, 2009).

———. Myth #62, "Canyon Confusion: Carson River not in Brunswick Canyon." Nevada State Library and Archives, Historical Myth a Month. www
.nevadaculture.org (accessed December 22, 2009).

———. Myth #79, "Nineteenth-Century Presidential Visits to Lake Tahoe and
Nevada." Nevada State Library and Archives, Historical Myth a Month.
www.nevadaculture.org (accessed December 22, 2009).

———. Myth #82, "Confusing Names: The Naming of Gardnerville." Nevada
State Library and Archives, Historical Myth a Month.
www.nevadaculture.org (accessed June 10, 2009).

———. Myth #108, "On the Edge: The Sierra Crest Line." Nevada State Library and Archives, Historical Myth a Month. www.nevadaculture.org (accessed December 22, 2009).

———. Myth #109, "U.S. Grant Did Not Get into Hot Water in Nevada." Nevada State Library and Archives, Historical Myth a Month. www .nevadaculture.org (accessed December 22, 2009).

———. Myth #111, "Riding High: Hank Monk and Horace Greeley." Nevada State Library and Archives, Historical Myth a Month. www.nevadaculture.org (accessed July 20, 2009).

———. Myth #114, "Carson City's Freeway Bypass: A Long Time Coming." Nevada State Library and Archives, Historical Myth a Month. www .nevadaculture.org (accessed June 10, 2009).

———. Myth #133, "Teddy Roosevelt was not at the Alamo (Stock Farm)." Nevada State Library and Archives, Historical Myth a Month. www.nevadaculture.org (accessed June 30, 2009).

———. Myth #143. "The Great Depression in Nevada." Nevada State Library and Archives, Historical Myth a Month. www.nevadaculture.org (accessed June 30, 2009).

———. Myth #148, "A Federal Case." Nevada State Library and Archives, Historical Myth a Month. www.nevadaculture.org (accessed December 22, 2009).

Schrantz, Scott. "Northern Nevada Then and Now," Photo #11, Central School, March 6, 2006. www.aroundcarson.com/thenandnow (accessed November 25, 2009).

Oral Histories

Calhoun, James W. *James W. Calhoun and the Nevada State Museum.* Reno: University of Nevada Oral History Program, 1987.

Crowell, Lucy Davis. *One Hundred Years at Nevada's Capital.* Reno: University of Nevada Oral History Program, 1965.

Graves, Richard L. *Take 'No' as a Starter—The Life of Richard L. Graves.* Reno: University of Nevada Oral History Program, 1980.

Guild, Clark J. *Clark J. Guild: Memoirs of Careers with Nevada Bench and Bar, Lyon County Offices, and the Nevada State Museum.* Reno: University of Nevada Oral History Program, 1967.

Sawyer, Grant. *Hang Tough!: Grant Sawyer, An Activist in the Governor's Mansion.* Reno: University of Nevada Oral History Program, 1993.

Winters, John D., and Kay. *JohnD and Kay Winters Oral History.* Carson City: Carson Preservation Coalition, 2002.

Unpublished Material

Chung, Sue Fawn. "Carson City's Chinatown." Speech delivered in Carson City at the dedication of the Chinatown plaque, October 31, 2003.

Earl, Phillip I. "U.S. Army transcontinental convoy." Unpublished account, 1999.

Manuscript Collections

Klein, Jacob. "Founders of Carson City." In *Nevada Historical Society Papers,* vol. 1, 1913–1916. Carson City: Nevada State Printing Office, 1883.

Nevers, Samuel A. "Nevada Pioneers." In *Nevada Historical Society Papers,* 1913–1916. Vol. 1. Carson City: Nevada State Printing Office, 1883.

Index